THE GIVE IT BACK THEORY

Kenyon R. Dudley, MHA

DP HOUSE
Dudley Publishing House
www.dudleypublishinghouse.net

DEDICATION

To those who have spent their lives carrying burdens that were never theirs to bear—this book is for you. May you find the courage to release, the strength to heal, and the freedom to live unburdened.

To my wife, Jasmine, my greatest partner in life and love— thank you for seeing me, for speaking truth when I was drowning, and for reminding me to give it back.

To my children, Reagan and Julian, may you always walk lightly, knowing you were created to stand free and whole.

To the One who gave me this revelation—God, my Father— all glory belongs to You.

TABLE OF CONTENTS

ACKNOWLEDGMENTS

First and foremost, I acknowledge God, my Father, who revealed *The Give It Back Theory* to me and carried me through my darkest days. Without Him, this book would not exist.

To my wife, Jasmine Dudley, my anchor and my greatest encourager—your unwavering love, wisdom, and strength have helped shape this message in ways words cannot express. Thank you for holding me up when I felt like I would fall.

To my children, Reagan and Julian, you are my greatest inspiration. Your joy and innocence remind me daily of the importance of releasing what isn't ours so we can embrace the fullness of life.

To all those along my journey—family, friends, mentors, and those who have walked beside me in moments of struggle and breakthrough—I honor you. Your stories, encouragement, and challenges have shaped this work.

To every reader, workshop attendee, and podcast listener—thank you for being part of this journey. May this book be the beginning of your freedom.

Now, let's give it back.

PREFACE

Life has a way of loading us up with burdens we didn't ask for. Growing up, I was deeply empathetic, almost painfully so. I couldn't help but absorb the emotions and experiences of others around me or on TV—the grief, the anger, the sorrow. For years, I thought it was my job to carry those burdens, to somehow fix the pain of everyone around me. I call it, *"The Savior Complex."* I had this constant urge to save others from their natural and eternal hell. But eventually, the weight of it all became too much.

Living like this caused me to have little breakdowns and bouts of depression throughout my years of growing, but nothing could've prepared me for what I was about to experience once I abruptly moved my wife and kids halfway across the country to another city at thrity-two years old. We had been so burdened by the responsibilities placed on us in our world back in our hometown, that we simply needed relief. So, after much prayer, we left Atlanta, Georgia and headed for Dallas, Texas. Each of us only having 2 bags. We gave up many things, and lost the rest back home in Atlanta. But none of that really mattered anymore. If we didn't move quick, someone was going to have a nervous breakdown. What I didn't know is that it was going to happen to the both of us—my wife and I— regardless of where we were.

I vividly remember one particular day that brought me to my breaking point. It scared the living daylights out of me. I was driving down a quiet North Dallas road when the enormity of everything I was carrying finally caught up with me. My chest felt tight, as though an invisible force was squeezing the air out of my lungs. My vision blurred, my heart pounded in my chest, and it felt like I was moments away from fainting. I struggled to catch my breath, gripping the wheel with trembling hands. It felt as if the world was closing in on me—as if I were dying right there behind the wheel. I didn't know it at the time, but I was experiencing a full-blown anxiety attack.

For years, I had been trying to live the lives of multiple people simultaneously: the perfect husband, father, and pastor, leader in Corporate America, entrepreneur, and friend. My new therapist summed it up perfectly: *"Kenyon, you're trying to live for too many people. You're exhausted."* I had thought that being everything to everyone was a badge of honor, but the truth was that I was overwhelmed, depleted, and suffocating under the weight of burdens I was never meant to carry.

That day on the side of the road, I realized something that changed my life forever: most of the pain and stress I was carrying didn't even belong to me. The grief, sadness, anger, rejection, abandonment, and frustration weren't mine; they were projections from others. And someway somehow, I had received those weights as my own. And in some regards, I had taken these burdens on without even being asked. My family's unresolved trauma, my friends' crises, societal expectations, and the heavy yoke of institutional demands from religion, education, and so many other places were all piled on my shoulders. And I had allowed it. But that day on the side of the road, with my heart racing and barely able to see or speak, I knew that I had to *give it all back*.

Now, I say that instinctively I knew that I had to give back the burdens of others, but the truth is I really didn't know that's what the action or decision was called. All I knew, was that most of the things I felt didn't even originate with me. It would eventually be my wife who helped me put words to this act of releasing pain and trauma that was not mine.

One day during one of my scary anxiety attack episodes she painfully and passionately yelled out, *"Kenyon! Give them folks their stuff back! This ain't even yours."* Though her passion helped me snap out of my trance and strengthened me to bring my entire being to a state of rest, I still hadn't quite gotten the concept of *"giving it back"* until one day I was listening to Oprah speak with Mel Robbins about her *"Let Them Theory"* on her Oprah Winfrey podcast. Mel's powerful revelation of allowing people to be who they really are, thrust me into a deeper revelation of my own. As I listened, I immediately knew that my issue was deeper than just controlling people because I felt I knew best. My arrogance and selfishness had a deeper reason. I knew that I was a genuine empathetic person, and my deepest fear was having to experience people in a state of anguish or pain. To me, that meant that I would have to experience this same anguish and pain by watching them go through it. The way my brain and heart was wired, I couldn't just *let* people suffer alone. But I didn't always know what to do with people's suffering. Often I would just internalize it and carry it with me. Hoping that the more I'd take it on, the less burden they'd have to feel. This would be a slow death had I kept going in this direction. I would have to *"let them,"* as Mel Robbins so eloquently speaks of in her theory. In order to *"let"* people be who they really are or experience their own journeys, I would have to actually do the work of *"giving them their life back."* That would include their trauma. This is what *"The Give It Back Theory"* is all about.

THE GIVE IT BACK THEORY

The *"Give It Back Theory"* is my way of helping you give people their struggle and trauma back. It's my way of helping you heal from second-hand trauma like I'm having to every day.

Most of the stress, anxiety, and pain we experience doesn't originate inside us—it's handed to us by external situations, circumstances, and people. Research in psychology calls this phenomenon *projection*: when individuals unconsciously transfer their emotions, traits, or unresolved issues onto others (Freud, 1920/2015). For empathetic people like myself, this often results in second-hand trauma—a condition where exposure to another person's pain or trauma causes emotional, psychological, or even physical distress (Figley, 1995). Studies have shown that second-hand trauma can mimic the symptoms of PTSD, including anxiety, depression, and chronic stress (Bride, 2007).

But it doesn't stop at psychological effects. Research indicates that prolonged exposure to second-hand trauma and chronic stress can lead to a host of physical health issues. The American Psychological Association (2021) reports that individuals experiencing chronic stress are at greater risk of heart disease, digestive problems, and weakened immune function. Chronic stress can also dysregulate the hypothalamic-pituitary-adrenal (HPA) axis, which governs our body's stress response, leading to long-term hormonal imbalances (McEwen & Gianaros, 2011).

Let me be clear: this isn't about avoiding responsibility or ignoring others' pain. It's about setting boundaries that protect your mental, emotional, and spiritual health. It's about releasing what doesn't serve you and reclaiming *your* identity, joy, and peace.

In this book, I'll share my journey—from carrying my family's trauma as a boy to navigating the expectations of the church, the entertainment industry, and even my wife's own dreams for me as a successful Black man. I'll introduce you to my theory of *"giving it back,"* and we'll explore eight practical and spiritual ways I personally use to release what's been placed on you by others. Along the way, I'll challenge you to embrace the process of letting go through reflection, prayer, and intentional action.

You'll also discover my *"10 Methods of Healing Yourself,"* a framework for restoring wholeness in every part of your being—mind, body, and spirit. These methods focus on different areas of the body where we store trauma: the head and neck, shoulders and chest, stomach and diaphragm, pelvis and hips, and legs and feet. Each chapter will guide you through recognizing, releasing, and healing the burdens stored in these areas.

Now, I don't claim to have all the answers. Healing is a process, and I'm still on the journey myself. But little by little, I've seen the power of *"giving it back"* in my own life. I've learned to return the grief, anger, and expectations to their rightful owners, and in doing so, I've reclaimed my identity and my peace.

This book isn't just a guide—it's an invitation. An invitation to step into the *weightless freedom* God intended for you. To confront the false burdens that have held you back and embrace the joy, wholeness, and purpose that are rightfully yours as child of God.

So, let's begin. Let's explore what it means to lay aside every weight that so easily entangles us and run the race marked out for us. *Let's give it all back, together.*

FOOTNOTES

1. Freud, S. (1920/2015). *Beyond the Pleasure Principle*. Martino Fine Books.

2. Figley, C. R. (1995). *Compassion Fatigue: Coping with Secondary Traumatic Stress Disorder in Those Who Treat the Traumatized*. Brunner/Mazel.

3. Bride, B. E. (2007). Prevalence of secondary traumatic stress among social workers. *Social Work*, 52(1), 63-70.

4. American Psychological Association. (2021). Stress effects on the body. Retrieved from www.apa.org

5. McEwen, B. S., & Gianaros, P. J. (2011). Stress- and allostasis-induced brain plasticity. *Annual Review of Medicine*, 62, 431-445.

SYNOPSIS OF PART I

UNDERSTANDING THE CONCEPT OF 'GIVING IT BACK'

P art I of *The Give It Back Theory* lays the foundation for understanding how we unconsciously carry burdens that were never ours to begin with. It explores the deep-rooted patterns of absorbing second-hand trauma, the ways projection impacts our mental and emotional well-being, and how unresolved pain can keep us stuck in cycles of arrested development. **This section is about *awareness*—**shining a light on the invisible weight many of us carry and preparing us to release it.

In Chapter 1: *My Empathic Journey*, I share my personal experiences as someone born with heightened empathy, detailing how my ability to feel others' emotions deeply led to enmeshment rather than true compassion. Through childhood experiences, including witnessing family conflicts and internalizing the emotional turmoil of those around me, I learned the dangers of caring without boundaries. This chapter reveals how many of us, especially those with empathetic tendencies, mistakenly believe that helping others means carrying their pain, which ultimately leads to emotional exhaustion and anxiety.

Chapter 2: *Second-Hand Trauma and Projection* introduces two key psychological concepts that are central to *The Give It Back Theory*. Second-hand trauma, also known as vicarious trauma, occurs when we absorb the emotional pain of others as if it were our own, leading to stress, anxiety, and even PTSD-like symptoms. Projection, on the other hand, is when others impose their unresolved fears, failures, and expectations onto us, making us feel responsible for emotions and struggles that were never ours to own. This chapter highlights how false burdens accumulate through relationships, work, and societal expectations, and how they shape our self-perception in damaging ways.

In Chapter 3: *Arrested Development*, I introduce the powerful concept that trauma—whether first-hand or second-hand—can stop us from growing emotionally, mentally, and spiritually at the very moment it entered our lives. This chapter recounts my revelation during an Uber ride, where a simple yet profound statement—*"Most people are stuck at the place the pain came upon them"*—shifted my perspective on healing. Rather than remaining trapped in the past, we can go back, recognize where we stopped growing, and *give back* the pain that is not ours. This chapter serves as a wake-up call, urging readers to release inherited struggles and break generational cycles.

Part I is designed to diagnose the problem—helping readers recognize how false burdens, second-hand trauma, and projection shape their lives. It sets the stage for Part II, where we begin learning how to give these burdens back and reclaim our freedom.

CHAPTER 1

MY EMPATHIC JOURNEY

S ome of us are born with unique gifts that set us apart from the beginning. For me, that gift was an overwhelming sense of empathy. I could feel the pain, joy, and struggles of others as though they were my own, and while this gift brought profound connection, it also came with an enormous weight I wasn't prepared to carry. I wasn't just observing other people's emotions—I was absorbing them, taking them into my own body, soul, and psyche. What I didn't realize until much later in life was that this pattern of carrying burdens that weren't mine would follow me well into adulthood.

Early Childhood: A Heart Too Open

My journey begins in the heart of a family weighed down by its own trauma. From an early age, I witnessed a revolving door of emotional pain within my household and my grandmother's. Family arguments, bona fide fights in the middle of my grandmother's street between family members, financial struggles, and unspoken grief seemed to fill every corner of our home and family. I didn't just notice these things; I internalized them. At five years old, I vividly remember sitting quietly at family gatherings, listening to adults talk about their problems as though I were their confidant. Back then, they didn't realize the weight their words and actions had on me. My little heart was too open, too attuned to their suffering.

There was one day I'll never forget—one that stays etched in my memory like a scar. I was playing at my grandmother's house when an argument broke out on the front porch. My uncle, fueled by anger, slapped my aunt, his wife, so hard that she fell into the big-screen television set. The entire household erupted into chaos—yelling, crying, fighting, and accusations flying in every direction. My mother and other aunts trying hard to pull my Uncle away from his wife. I remember standing there, frozen, unable to process the violence and confusion. I carried that pain, that fear, and that chaos in my spirit for decades, all the way into my marriage, not realizing how deeply it had affected me.

It wasn't just the adults. My empathy extended to my siblings and neighborhood friends. If someone cried, I cried. If someone was angry, I felt it like fire in my chest. I didn't have the language to explain it at the time, but I felt like a mirror, reflecting everyone else's emotions back to them. And while this gave me a certain prophetic edge and wisdom beyond my years, it also made me an easy target for emotional overload. What I didn't understand then was how to *care without carrying.* I thought that in order to truly help someone, I had to take on their burden as my own. This misunderstanding is common among those with high empathy, as research shows that overly empathetic individuals often struggle with distinguishing their own emotions from those of others (Neff & Germer, 2018).

The Weight of Family Trauma

One of the most vivid memories of my childhood involved my mother's quiet grief and loud anger. She carried a burden that was too heavy for one person, shaped by the trauma of her own upbringing and the demands of raising children on her own for many years. I would later find out that I was the child that she was ashamed of because of being conceived by a man who had not yet finalized his divorce from his previous wife. She had been lied to by my father, and she unknowingly dated a man who was still married. I often heard her crying late at night behind closed doors, and though she tried to shield us from her pain, I felt it deeply. Her sadness became my sadness, and her unspoken fears and anger became my own.

In my extended family, dysfunction was a familiar pattern. Heated arguments could erupt without warning, and moments of joy often felt fleeting. I vividly remember watching two of my uncles argue so intensely that fists flew and they fell down my grandmother's front steps into her bushes, shattering the fragile illusion of familial peace.

It wasn't just the acts of violence I witnessed—it was the aftermath that lingered. The silence that followed, the unspoken agreement not to talk about it, and the weight of unresolved conflict became mine to carry. This aligns with findings that children who witness familial conflict often internalize emotional turmoil, leading to chronic stress and anxiety in adulthood (McEwen, 2008).

These moments taught me a warped version of empathy—one where I believed it was my job to hold the family's pain, to somehow fix what was broken. I didn't yet understand that **empathy doesn't require enmeshment.** Bearing one another's burdens isn't about taking on someone else's responsibility to heal; it's about being a support system while allowing them the space to grow, struggle, and learn for themselves (Galatians 6:2).

The Breaking Point

Fast-forward to adulthood, when I moved to Texas with my wife and kids. This move was meant to be a fresh start for us, a chance to build a life filled with hope and promise without weights or distractions. But as I settled into this new chapter, I began to realize how much emotional baggage I had brought with me. The stress of balancing family life, work, and ministry all while rebuilding and enduring pain from old hurts and letdowns amplified the unresolved emotions I had been carrying since childhood.

It all came to a head that day I was driving down that quiet road in North Dallas. My chest felt so tight, like an anaconda was squeezing the life out of me from the inside. And tears I couldn't explain flowed from my blurry and weary eyes. In that moment, it dawned on me that the pain and weight I had been feeling weren't just my own—they were the accumulated burdens of everyone and everything I had ever cared about. I had spent my entire life being a sponge for other people's emotions, and it was draining the life out of me.

Compassion vs. Enmeshment

It would be over a year later that I realized I couldn't continue to carry what wasn't mine. I needed to *"give it back."* The concept wasn't about rejecting people or their pain, but about drawing a clear boundary between compassion and enmeshment. I realized that empathy didn't mean I had to internalize someone else's struggles. I could care deeply for others without losing myself in the process.

"Giving it back" became my survival mechanism. Whenever I felt the weight of someone else's emotions or external forces pressing down on me, I would pause, reflect, breathe, and intentionally release it by saying, *"I'm giving it back."* Sometimes this meant continuing on in prayer after uttering those transformative words, asking God to lift the burden and carry it for me and for those to whom the burden originally belonged. Other times it meant having honest conversations with myself, reminding myself, *"This isn't mine to hold."*

Practicing compassion without enmeshment looks like this: listening without absorbing, offering support without over-identifying, and recognizing where your responsibility ends and someone else's begins. It's showing up for someone without trying to rescue them. It's praying for someone without internalizing their pain as your own. This balance has been one of the hardest but most rewarding lessons of my life.

Over time, I began to see how this practice allowed me to thrive. Instead of being crushed by the weight of the world, I found a way to stand still and tall. *"Giving it back"* didn't mean I stopped caring—in fact, it allowed me to care more authentically. I could show up for others without being consumed by their struggles. It was so liberating.

Embracing The Gift

Looking back, I see how my heightened sense of empathy shaped every facet of my life. It made me a better husband, father, friend, and leader. But it also taught me the importance of boundaries. Empathy is a gift, but like any gift, it must be stewarded wisely. Without boundaries, it can become a curse, leaving you depleted and resentful.

Today, I embrace my empathy as a divine gift, one that allows me to connect deeply with others. But I also recognize that it comes with a responsibility: to protect my own heart while being a vessel of love and compassion for those around me. *"Giving it back"* isn't just a survival mechanism; it's a way of thriving, a path to living fully and authentically.

This chapter is a piece of my story, but if you're reading this, I believe it's also yours. If you've ever felt overwhelmed by the weight of other people's emotions or external forces such as the culture or institutions, know that you're not alone. And know that it's okay to *"give it back."* In fact, it's necessary. Because only when you release what isn't yours can you truly carry what is meant for you.

FOOTNOTES

1. Neff, K. D., & Germer, C. K. (2018). *The mindful self-compassion workbook: A proven way to accept yourself, build inner strength, and thrive.* The Guilford Press.

2. McEwen, B. S. (2008). Central effects of stress hormones in health and disease: Understanding the protective and damaging effects of stress and stress mediators. *European Journal of Pharmacology*, 583(2-3), 174-185.

3. Galatians 6:2, Holy Bible, New International Version.

CHAPTER 2

SECOND-HAND TRAUMA AND PROJECTION

Have you ever walked into a room and felt like you were hit by a wave of someone else's bad mood? Or maybe you've had a conversation with a friend where they unload all their problems, and you leave feeling emotionally drained, like you've somehow taken on their struggles. That's second-hand trauma and projection at work—when people offload their grief, sadness, frustration, or even identity burdens onto you, whether you signed up for it or not. It's messy, exhausting, and often unintentional, but it can wreak havoc on your mental, physical, and spiritual well-being if left unchecked.

What Is Second-Hand Trauma?

Second-hand trauma, also known as vicarious trauma, occurs when you experience emotional or psychological distress due to exposure to someone else's trauma (Figley, 1995). This isn't about having a bad day because your coworker told you their cat is sick. No, this is the deep stuff—the kind of pain that seeps into your soul and keeps you up at night, replaying someone else's wounds as if they were your own.

Take my own life as an example. Growing up, I was the designated "listener" in my family. When adults in my family fought, cried, or vented about their struggles, I absorbed it all. I wasn't just hearing their words; I was living their pain. My uncles' and aunts' outbursts of anger, my grandmother's sadness and despair, my mother's silent grief, my siblings' and cousins' rebellions and struggles were all imprinted on me. At the time, I didn't realize this was second-hand trauma—I just thought I was being a "good son" or a "mature kid." But as I got older, I began to see how carrying these emotional weights was slowly eroding my own sense of self.

Real-world examples of second-hand trauma are often seen in leadership, service, and caregiving professions. A nurse in an ICU, for instance, may develop symptoms of secondary traumatic stress simply by witnessing the pain and suffering of patients and their families daily. Teachers in underfunded schools often report high levels of emotional burnout because they're exposed to the struggles of students navigating poverty and trauma at home (American Psychological Association, 2021). Even close relationships can create second-hand trauma—such as when one partner constantly absorbs the stress and unresolved issues of the other.

The Projection Connection

Closely tied to second-hand trauma is projection. In psychological terms, projection happens when someone unconsciously attributes their own unwanted feelings, desires, or traits onto another person (Freud, 1920/2015). Think of it like a game of emotional dodgeball, except you're the only player being pelted with balls labeled "insecurity," "anger," "fear," and so on.

For example, I vividly remember a family member telling me, *"You're going to be the one who saves this family."* At first, it felt like a compliment, a noble mission even. But as I grew older, I realized that what they were really saying was, *"I'm projecting my unmet expectations and unresolved issues about family onto you."* The pressure to *"save"* everyone became a heavy burden that wasn't mine to carry.

Projection in professional settings can also take a toll. A manager who is insecure about their leadership abilities might criticize their team for being *"unorganized"* or *"inefficient,"* when in reality, they're projecting their own self-doubt. Similarly, in families, a parent who never achieved their dreams might project their unfulfilled ambitions onto their child, creating immense pressure for the child to succeed. Either way, projection is beyond unbearable when you're the receipient of it.

Empathy vs. Enmeshment

Here's where it gets tricky. As someone with heightened empathy, I've always felt deeply for others. But there's a fine line between empathy and enmeshment. Empathy is about understanding and caring for someone else's emotions; enmeshment is about internalizing them to the point where you lose sight of where they end and you begin (Neff & Germer, 2018).

Let me break it down a little more. Imagine empathy as offering someone a tissue when they're crying. Enmeshment, on the other hand, is when you take the tissue, blow your own nose, and start crying along with them. It's messy, unhelpful, it's unhealthy, and completely unsustainable. Eventually, you'll burn out, get infected with the same *dis*-ease, or worse. You'll become something or someone that you don't even recognize.

In my own life, I often blurred this line. When a friend confided in me about their financial struggles, I didn't just sympathize—I took on their anxiety as if my bank account was also in the red. When a mentor expressed frustration with their career, I felt it in my chest like it was my problem to solve. It took years of reflection, therapy, and hitting hard times to understand that I could be compassionate without becoming consumed.

Research confirms this distinction. Compassion, defined as an empathetic concern coupled with a desire to help, is linked to better mental health outcomes. However, enmeshment, or excessive identification with another person's emotions, has been shown to increase stress and emotional exhaustion, particularly in familial and caregiving relationships (Singer & Klimecki, 2014).

Research Backs It Up

Studies have shown that second-hand trauma and projection can have profound effects on mental and physical health. The American Psychological Association (2021) highlights that individuals exposed to second-hand trauma are at increased risk for anxiety, depression, and even PTSD-like symptoms. Chronic exposure can also lead to weariness and fatigue, especially for those in caregiving roles (Bride, 2007).

For instance, mental health professionals often report experiencing *"compassion fatigue,"* a condition that mirrors the symptoms of PTSD, as a result of prolonged exposure to their clients' traumatic experiences (Figley, 1995). Similarly, children who grow up in high-conflict households are more likely to develop second-hand trauma, as they absorb the stress and unresolved conflicts of their parents (McEwen, 2008).

Projection, too, can be insidious. When people project their insecurities or unresolved emotions onto you, it can distort your own self-perception. Over time, you might start to believe the labels others place on you, even if they're completely unfounded. For example, being called *"the troublemaker"* as a child might lead you to internalize feelings of guilt or inadequacy, shaping how you see yourself well into adulthood. In workplace settings, projection can create toxic environments, where employees are unfairly blamed for issues that stem from leadership insecurities (Neff & Germer, 2018). It's something that you must be aware of at all times, because it's easy to blur the lines and be living out someone else's life.

Breaking the Cycle

So, how do we break free from the grip of second-hand trauma and projection? It starts with awareness. You know, that thing that's happening to your brain and heart right now. When you recognize when someone is projecting their emotions onto you, remind yourself that *their* feelings are not *your* responsibility. Practice self-compassion, as this can help you set healthier boundaries and separate your emotions from others' (Neff & Germer, 2018).

Another key step is learning to say *"no"* without guilt. Ok, I know you've heard this before. But it's true, *"No,"* is a full sentence. You don't have to explain or rationalize your *"no."* If it doesn't feel right to you, or if you immediately feel pressured, say, *"No."* This doesn't mean you stop caring; it means you care enough about yourself to prioritize your well-being. Saying, *"No,"* to someone's emotional baggage doesn't make you a bad person—it makes you a healthy one.

Finally, find humor in the absurdity of it all. Life is too short to carry every ringmaster and their circus on your back. When someone tries to hand you their emotional baggage, picture yourself holding up a *"closed for business"* sign. It's okay to step back, breathe, and focus on your own emotional health. And if you just so happen to pick it up unconsciously, always know that you can say those three supernatural words that will break the grip off your mind, body, and soul: *"Give it back."*

Moving Forward

Second-hand trauma and projection are sneaky thieves that steal your peace, but they don't have to define your story. By recognizing these patterns, setting boundaries, and practicing self-compassion, you can reclaim your sense of self and thrive. Remember, it's not your job to save everyone or live up to someone else's projections. Your only job is to be authentically you—and that's more than enough.

FOOTNOTES

1. Figley, C. R. (1995). *Compassion Fatigue: Coping with Secondary Traumatic Stress Disorder in Those Who Treat the Traumatized.* Brunner/Mazel.

2. Freud, S. (1920/2015). *Beyond the Pleasure Principle.* Martino Fine Books.

3. Neff, K. D., & Germer, C. K. (2018). *The mindful self-compassion workbook: A proven way to accept yourself, build inner strength, and thrive.* The Guilford Press.

4. Bride, B. E. (2007). Prevalence of secondary traumatic stress among social workers. *Social Work*, 52(1), 63-70.

5. McEwen, B. S. (2008). Central effects of stress hormones in health and disease: Understanding the protective and damaging effects of stress and stress mediators. *European Journal of Pharmacology*, 583(2-3), 174-185.

6. Singer, T., & Klimecki, O. M. (2014). Empathy and compassion. *Current Biology*, 24(18), R875-R878.

7. American Psychological Association. (2021). Stress effects on the body. Retrieved from www.apa.org

CHAPTER 3

ARRESTED DEVELOPMENT

There comes a time in everyone's life when trauma, disappointment, or fear creates an invisible wall between who they are and who they were meant to be. For some, it happens in childhood. For others, it's a moment in adulthood when everything seems to freeze in place. This is what we call **arrested development**—the phenomenon of stopping emotionally, mentally, and spiritually at the very point where pain entered your life. Instead of growing beyond the moment, people become stuck in it, whether consciously or unconsciously (Van der Kolk, 2014). But what if instead of giving up and being stuck, we could *give it back* so we can keep elevating?

The Revelation in an Uber Ride

I was catching an Uber from my office one day. It had been an extremely long and tiresome day, and I wasn't in the greatest of moods. Then, an old, beat-up black Nissan Altima pulled up to pick me up. When I got in, I saw a woman in the driver's seat,

17

dressed casually with her hair pinned up. She looked to be in her late 40s or 50s. It was a Friday night, and all I wanted to do was push through North Dallas traffic and get home to my family. My son had just been released from the hospital after surgery, my wife—who had been tirelessly caring for him while balancing work and coaching clients—needed my help at home, and my daughter was waiting for Daddy to get home so she could tell me all about her day.

I was exhausted, weighed down with negative thoughts and emotions. The battle against negative thoughts and emotions in the backdrop of my mind throughout the day wasn't unusual for me. But for some reason, God orchestrated for me to be picked up by this particular lady that evening. Her spirit of gratitude and excitement was infectious. Despite my fatigue and the mental battle, I couldn't help but engage with her in conversation. Though I wrestle, I can discern quite well. It's in my nature to see the good in people.

As we talked, I felt God whisper that she was about to give me an answer from Him that I needed to hear. About twenty minutes into the ride, she said something that stopped me in my tracks: *"Mr. Kenyon,"* she said, *"So many people are walking around sad, angry, frustrated, and on guard."*

I looked at her through the rearview mirror—knowing this was God's invitation for me to engage—and responded, *"That's because more than half the world is traumatized."*

She burst with energy and excitement, as she agreement with the revelation. So, I went further. I told her, **"According to** *research, approximately 70% of people globally are estimated to have experienced a traumatic event in their lifetime. And while there's no exact figure for those experiencing second-hand trauma, studies suggest that a significant portion of people who are closely connected to someone who has experienced trauma may develop symptoms of secondary traumatic stress—particularly individuals in service and caregiving professions like therapists, healthcare workers, or even family members"* (Branson & Baetz, 2017).

At this point, the woman almost leaped out of the driver's seat with excitement. Then she said the words that would shape the foundation of this book: ***"It's called arrested development. Most people are stuck at the very place the pain came upon them"*** (Perry, 2006).

That was it! That was the answer I had been seeking. We stop growing at the exact moment trauma enters our lives, and instead of pushing past it, we freeze. Instead of throwing our hands up in surrender and healing, we throw our hands up in defeat. But what if we could change that? What if, instead of staying stuck, we could *give it back?*

Breaking the Cycle: The Arrest Stops With You

If you're reading this, I want you to do something right now. Hold your hands up, close your eyes, and go back to that moment—the moment where you stopped growing, the moment you were hurt, the moment trauma locked you in place. Now say to yourself: ***"I'm giving it back, and I'm growing*** *beyond from this"* (Siegel, 2012). Say it as many times as you need to. Say it until you begin to feel the release of burdens and weights in your soul and body.

Truth is, arrested development doesn't just come from first-hand trauma. Much of it comes from **second-hand trauma**— the pain and burdens projected onto us by others. It's generational trauma. It's shared trauma. And many times, it's communal (collective) trauma. But hear me: **the arrest stops with you. The freedom begins with you.**

Entire bloodlines, families, groups, and communities have been caught in cycles of arrested development. Some people are still carrying their grandfather's trauma. Some communities are still suffering from historical wounds that haven't been healed. But **you can be the one who stops the cycle** (Felitti et al., 1998). **You can be the one who says, *"No more."***

The Exchange: Letting Go and Moving Forward

The only way to move forward is to make an exchange. You must go back to that place of pain—as often as necessary—to put your hands up in surrender, and say: *"I will exchange holding onto this pain. I will give it back to whoever or whatever traumatized me. And in return, I will take back my soul, my identity, my growth, and my future."*

I know this isn't easy. Tell me about it. Trauma has a way of embedding itself into our very being, making us believe that we are our wounds. But we are not. **You are not what happened to you. You are not the pain you endured. You are not the** disappointment, the abuse, the neglect, the fear. **You are bigger than all of it** (Gabor, 2021).

Your Freedom is Connected to Others

I need you to understand something: **Your freedom isn't just about you.** When you grow beyond your arrested development, you create space for others to do the same. Your children, your spouse, your friends, your community—everyone around you benefits when you break free.

When you heal, you disrupt the cycle of generational trauma. When you choose to give back the burdens that were never yours to carry, you create a ripple effect that extends beyond yourself. Your healing becomes permission for others to heal. Your growth becomes a testimony that inspires others to grow.

The arrest stops here. The freedom starts with you. Let's venture beyond this point in the book. I want to show you exactly how I've worked day-in and day-out to move beyond the traumatic pit that I was in.

FOOTNOTES

1. Van der Kolk, B. (2014). *The body keeps the score: Brain, mind, and body in the healing of trauma*. Penguin Publishing Group.

2. Branson, D. C., & Baetz, C. L. (2017). Secondary traumatic stress in mental health professionals: Risk factors and strategies for prevention. *Journal of Traumatic Stress*, 30(2), 235-242.

3. Perry, B. D. (2006). *The boy who was raised as a dog: And other stories from a child psychiatrist's notebook*. Basic Books.

4. Siegel, D. J. (2012). *The developing mind: How relationships and the brain interact to shape who we are*. Guilford Press.

5. Felitti, V. J., Anda, R. F., Nordenberg, D., Williamson, D. F., Spitz, A. M., Edwards, V., Koss, M. P., & Marks, J. S. (1998). Relationship of childhood abuse and household dysfunction to many of the leading causes of death in adults. *American Journal of Preventive Medicine*, 14(4), 245-258.

6. Gabor, M. (2021). *The myth of normal: Trauma, illness, and healing in a toxic culture*. Avery Publishing.

SYNOPSIS OF PART II

THE FOUNDATION OF 'GIVE IT BACK'

P art II serves as the blueprint for releasing false burdens, providing readers with the spiritual, psychological, and practical tools to actively give back what was never theirs. This section shifts from understanding *why* we carry emotional weight to learning *how* to set it down. Here, I introduce the structured *"8 Ways to Give It Back"*, showing readers how to practice healthy emotional and spiritual boundaries.

Chapter 4: *A Transformative Formula for Freedom* sets the tone for this section, explaining why *giving back* is essential for personal growth. Using the scriptural principle of laying aside every weight (Hebrews 12:1) and research on stress and trauma, this chapter bridges the gap between spiritual wisdom and psychological science. It presents the necessity of detachment, healing rituals, and the decision to release inherited pain as foundational steps toward true emotional freedom.

Chapter 5: *Introducing the 8 Ways to 'Give It Back'* introduces the core methodology of this book, detailing eight actionable strategies for returning false burdens:

1. Boundary Acknowledgment – Recognizing what is yours to carry versus what belongs to others.

2. Name It to Tame It – Identifying emotions and projections so they no longer hold power over you.

3. Reframing & Release Rituals – Engaging in symbolic acts (e.g., letter-burning, journaling) to let go.

4. Empathetic Detachment – Learning to care without absorbing others' pain.

5. Prayer & Meditation – Using spiritual practices to release burdens to God.

6. Physical Realignment – Understanding how trauma is stored in the body and moving it out.

7. Community Accountability – Surrounding yourself with people who reinforce healthy boundaries.

8. Ongoing Maintenance – Committing to daily check-ins to ensure you don't pick up new burdens.

Chapter 6: *Pick Up the Rug* is a powerful metaphor for what happens when we suppress pain instead of dealing with it. Using my personal story of physical illness following trauma, I explain how unresolved emotional burdens manifest in our bodies as weights, often leading to chronic illness, stress, and fatigue. Healing begins when we lift the rug, confront what's beneath, and intentionally shake out what doesn't belong to us.

Part II transitions readers from *awareness* to *action*, laying the groundwork for daily practices that help restore clarity, emotional balance, and spiritual renewal. Here we go!

CHAPTER 4

A TRANSFORMATIVE FORMULA

FOR FREEDOM

We start taking our life back the moment we begin to release the burdens given to us. I call them "false burdens," because they don't originate with you. Releasing false burdens isn't just about lightening your emotional load though—it's about stepping into a healthier, truer version of yourself. This process is grounded in both spiritual truths and psychological principles, which, when combined, offer a transformative path toward freedom and wholeness.

The Sacred Call to Release

"Therefore, since we are surrounded by such a great cloud of witnesses, let us lay aside every weight and the sin that so easily entangles, and let us run with endurance the race that is set before us" (Hebrews 12:1). Before we move deeper into this thought, it's imperative that we realize what "sin" is. I don't want you to read this scripture through the lens of religion. Sin is not just the wrongdoing that a loving God wants to punish you for. That's religion. The

25

higher definition is this: sin is anything that **separates** us from the presence, power, and peace of God. This verse from the Holy Bible serves as a powerful reminder that we are not meant to carry unnecessary weights—emotional, spiritual, ours, theirs, or otherwise. We weren't built for that. We weren't built to carry anyone. We were only built with the capacity to care and have compassion for everyone. The race of life demands our focus and energy. It takes focus and energy (power; your God-given power) to properly care for someone or something. That, my friend, is much of the reason you were born. That is your purpose. But we cannot run our set race of life effectively or purposefully if we are burdened by false identities, second-hand trauma, and unresolved projections.

Throughout history, religious and spiritual traditions across the world have emphasized the necessity of releasing burdens. In Christianity, surrendering to God and casting our anxieties upon Him (1 Peter 5:7) is an act of faith and healing. Buddhism speaks of detachment and the letting go of suffering through mindfulness and acceptance (Kabat-Zinn, 1990). Hinduism encourages the relinquishment of karma and burdens to divine wisdom, while Indigenous cultures perform ceremonial cleansings and storytelling as methods of releasing inherited trauma (Duran, 2006). **The overarching spiritual principle is clear: trauma happens in the spirit first and manifests in the physical second.** So if you want to heal the physical, you're going to have to start with the spirit. That's where the trauma happened first.

This understanding is what makes the field of psychology so powerful and necessary. And it's one of the reasons I've been so fascinated with this industry. Contrary to what many believe, I believe that psychology is spiritual. Trauma, whether first-hand or second-hand, affects the neural pathways of the brain (Van der Kolk, 2014). It stores itself in our bodies, impacting emotions, behaviors, and even physical health. Psychology operates on the fundamental truth that healing begins with awareness, detachment, and restructuring thought patterns— principles that have been echoed in spiritual traditions for centuries. In this way, spirituality and psychology are not at odds but complementary; and maybe even synonymous in some ways.

When we release false burdens, we engage in a deeply spiritual and psychological transformation, actively rewriting the script of our lives and shedding the weight of inherited traumas. That's spiritual work. Releasing doesn't mean forgetting or ignoring; it just means that you're confronting, processing, and surrendering that which no longer serves us.

The Disney Audition

One of the most vivid examples of weights I had to release happened when I was just a teenager. The weights I carried kept me from walking into an opportunity of a lifetime. At just sixteen years old, I had moved across the country—from Atlanta to Los Angeles—to pursue my acting and singing dreams. It was after being discovered at a talent expo in Las Vegas, that this opportunity came to me. Living in L.A. was a whirlwind—a mix of excitement and homesickness—and it came with immense pressure. By the time I was seventeen or eighteen years old, I found myself in the middle of one of the biggest opportunities of my young career: a chance to audition for a major Disney television show.

It was close to Christmas, and the town had shut down for the season. I had gone back to Atlanta to spend the holidays with my family. Nursing my homesick heart, I savored every moment of being home. While enjoying my family, I received the call that I needed to return to L.A. the very next day to complete the final round of auditions for this Disney role I was up for. If I remember correctly, I had been through almost eight rounds of auditions for this part and it had gotten down to me and one other guy who was up for the role. This wasn't just any role—it was a kid-hosting job that would pay me more than I had ever seen at the time and it would literally take me around the world. The weight of the moment felt unbearable and frightening.

I could feel my mother's fear and sadness as she watched me rush to prepare to leave again. She wanted the best for me, but I could see the hesitation in her eyes. She had never traveled anywhere other than Florida before my entertainment career began, and the thought of me landing an acting job that would require international travel was overwhelming for her too. For me, the anxiety of the moment was compounded by the loneliness of traveling back to L.A. alone. I was staying with my manager at the time, and while they were supportive, it wasn't the same as having family nearby. Up to the point of me moving to L.A., my family and I had never been apart.

The weight of my mother's anxiety, hope, and fear. The weight of the expectations of my team, the excitement and hope of my extended family and church family. The burden of my own dreams and fears all wrapped in one felt like too much for a teenager to bear. I walked into that audition room carrying the unspoken traumas and fears of my family; many of which had I unknowingly adopted as my own. Not only that, but I walked in with the pressure to succeed. And I blew it. I let the anxiety, the trauma, and fears consume me. The entire audition was perfect, until the very end. The producers asked me one question, and I blew it...intentionally. Walking out of that room, I knew I didn't get the job. And I was filled with regret and shame that stayed with me for years.

Days later, I heard that the guy I was up against would be playing the role that part of me desperately wanted but was too afraid and traumatized to rise up and secure. The truth is, while standing in that room, I thought about what my mother would think if I left her. After all, I was her only son. Who would be her listening ear? Who would have talks with her about God, and help her see things differently? Who would help her pray or go rescue a family member in need? I had been that child for her since I was a boy. Then I thought of my aunt who was pastoring our home-church at the time. Who would help her with the church? After all, I was the young protégé preacher coming up in the family that was supposed to take on the family ministry. If my career exploded now, who would be there to take over the ministry? Then I thought, well, who would travel with me? I knew my father wasn't particularly interested in flying or leaving Georgia. Plus, he was already falling ill. He couldn't possibly go with me. And I knew my mother wasn't going to leave Atlanta for so many reasons like fear of travelling around the world, fear of leaving her mother and ill husband behind, fear of leaving the operations of their company in the hands of anyone else, and so much more.

These thoughts and a million more flooded my head at the end of that audition. I knew that if I had answered that last question correctly, then I would be around the world in a flash. But I was too afraid to leave my family. The false burdens that had been placed on me by others and myself stood in the way of my destiny. And for years, I carried the weight of regret.

It took extensive healing work to release the burden of that experience, and the weights that were revealed to me while in that moment. The hardest part wasn't forgiving myself though—it was releasing the false belief that I had let everyone down, and releasing the lie that I had to stay close to my family because they needed me. Those two conflicting false burdens zapped me of the hope of succeeding for years. And I had to go to the spiritual and psychological depths to reclaim my joy, my peace, my freedom, and my own identity.

Moving Forward

Releasing false burdens is both a spiritual practice and a psychological process. And it is the transformative formula you need to reclaim your freedom. This formula requires us to trust in God's sovereignty while also doing the inner work of challenging distorted beliefs and setting healthy boundaries. By aligning spiritual truths with psychological tools, we can move from a life weighed down by false identities to one marked by peace, authenticity, and resilience.

As you continue this journey, remember: you were never meant to carry the weight of the world. By laying aside every weight and embracing your true identity, you can run the race set before you with endurance, joy, and freedom.

FOOTNOTES

1. Kabat-Zinn, J. (1990). *Full catastrophe living: Using the wisdom of your body and mind to face stress, pain, and illness.* Delacorte.

2. Van der Kolk, B. (2014). *The body keeps the score: Brain, mind, and body in the healing of trauma.* Penguin Publishing Group.

3. Duran, E. (2006). *Healing the soul wound: Counseling with American Indians and other native peoples.* Teachers College Press.

4. Beck, A. T. (1976). *Cognitive therapy and the emotional disorders.* International Universities Press.

5. Cloud, H., & Townsend, J. (1992). *Boundaries: When to say yes, how to say no to take control of your life.* Zondervan.

CHAPTER 5

INTRODUCING THE 8 WAYS TO 'GIVE IT BACK'

Releasing false burdens is not a one-time event but an ongoing practice. In this chapter, we introduce eight foundational methods for *giving back* the emotional and mental weight that was never meant to be yours. Each method is a tool that allows you to redefine what you carry, reclaim your peace, and create healthy boundaries in your life. These eight approaches are designed to help you recognize, release, and redirect burdens in a way that aligns with both spiritual and psychological healing.

1. Boundary Acknowledgment: Clearly Identifying What is Yours and What is Theirs

The first step in *giving it back* is recognizing what belongs to you and what belongs to someone else. Many people struggle with setting healthy boundaries, often taking on responsibilities, emotions, and expectations that aren't their own (Cloud &

Townsend, 1992). Boundaries protect your mental and emotional well-being and provide clarity on what is truly within your control.

A helpful exercise is to visualize two baskets—one labeled *Mine* and the other *Not Mine*. Each time you feel overwhelmed, ask yourself: *Is this burden mine to carry?* If not, release it into the *"Not Mine"* basket.

2. Name It to Tame It: Recognizing the Emotion or Projection So You Can Give It Back

Naming emotions is a powerful psychological tool for reducing their intensity. Studies show that labeling emotions activates the brain's regulatory processes, allowing for a more balanced response to stress (Lieberman et al., 2007). When you feel overwhelmed, pause and name the emotion: *Is this mine, or has it been projected onto me?*

Remember, projection occurs when others impose their fears, anxieties, or expectations onto you. By recognizing when this is happening, you can stop internalizing these burdens and consciously *give them back*.

3. Reframing & Release Rituals: Simple Practices Like Writing Letters or Performing Symbolic Acts

Symbolic acts of release have been practiced across cultures for centuries. Whether it's writing a letter you never send, burning a list of grievances, or physically throwing a stone into a river to represent letting go, these rituals help shift subconscious emotional attachments (Pennebaker, 1997). The act of externalizing and releasing stored emotions creates psychological closure.

Consider setting aside time each month to perform a ritual of release—whether through journaling, lighting a candle, or practicing a symbolic gesture of giving back what is not yours to hold. I do my practices each week. You can set your own time cadence of when you perform outward release rituals. Ensure that it's scheduled during a time you will most likely keep up with considering your life's demands.

4. Empathetic Detachment: Caring Without Carrying

Empathy allows us to connect deeply with others, but unchecked empathy can lead to enmeshment—where you carry someone else's burdens as if they were your own (Neff & Germer, 2018). Learning to practice empathetic detachment enables you to offer support without absorbing another's pain.

A helpful mantra is: *I can care deeply while allowing them to own their journey.* Visualizing yourself as a supportive observer rather than an emotional sponge helps establish emotional distance while maintaining compassion.

5. Prayer & Meditation: Spiritual Tools to Release and Receive Peace

Spiritual practices such as prayer and meditation create intentional moments for surrendering burdens. Studies indicate that mindfulness meditation reduces stress and improves emotional regulation (Kabat-Zinn, 1990). Likewise, scripture encourages believers to "Cast all your anxieties on Him

[Almighty God] because He [Almighty God] cares for you" (1 Peter 5:7).

Through prayer, we engage in divine exchange—handing over worries and receiving peace in return. Similarly, mindfulness meditation allows for detachment from distressing emotions, cultivating a state of grounded presence.

6. Physical Realignment: Understanding How the Body Stores Stress and Tension

Trauma and stress are stored in the body, manifesting in muscle tension, digestive issues, and chronic pain (Van der Kolk, 2014). Somatic healing techniques, such as stretching, deep breathing, movement-based therapy, even chiropractic services, allow for the physical release of stored burdens.

Practices such as a deep-tissue massage, and intentional breathwork signal the nervous system that it is safe to let go. Consider incorporating body-based exercises into your routine to aid in the physical aspect of giving back what doesn't belong to you.

7. Community Accountability: Surrounding Yourself with People Who Recognize and Support Your Boundaries

Healing is not meant to be done in isolation. Surrounding yourself with a supportive community ensures that you remain accountable for maintaining boundaries and prioritizing self-care (Brown, 2010). Trusted friends, mentors, or faith-based groups can provide encouragement and reinforcement as you practice giving back what was never yours to carry.

Find a group or an individual who understands your healing journey. Verbalizing what you are giving back and receiving encouragement can reinforce your commitment to this process.

8. Ongoing Maintenance: Daily Check-ins and Self-Care Strategies

Healing is a lifelong journey, requiring consistent maintenance. Daily check-ins—whether through journaling, prayer, or simple self-reflection—help prevent new burdens from accumulating (Siegel, 2012). Developing routines for self-care, including exercise, rest, and mindfulness, strengthens resilience and sustains emotional health.

At the end of each day, take a moment to reflect: *What am I carrying that isn't mine?* Release it before going to sleep, ensuring that you wake up lighter and more at peace.

These eight methods offer a structured way to *give back* what does not belong to you. Each approach provides a practical tool for shifting burdens and embracing a life of greater peace and clarity. As we move forward, we will explore each of these methods in depth, offering practical exercises, real-life applications, and spiritual insights for lasting transformation.

FOOTNOTES

1. Cloud, H., & Townsend, J. (1992). *Boundaries: When to say yes, how to say no to take control of your life.* Zondervan.

2. Lieberman, M. D., Eisenberger, N. I., Crockett, M. J., Tom, S. M., Pfeifer, J. H., & Way, B. M. (2007). Putting feelings into words: Affect labeling disrupts amygdala activity in response to affective stimuli. *Psychological Science,* 18(5), 421-428.

3. Pennebaker, J. W. (1997). *Opening up: The healing power of expressing emotions.* Guilford Press.

4. Neff, K. D., & Germer, C. K. (2018). *The mindful self-compassion workbook: A proven way to accept yourself, build inner strength, and thrive.* The Guilford Press.

5. Kabat-Zinn, J. (1990). *Full catastrophe living: Using the wisdom of your body and mind to face stress, pain, and illness.* Delacorte.

6. Van der Kolk, B. (2014). *The body keeps the score: Brain, mind, and body in the healing of trauma.* Penguin Publishing Group.

7. Brown, B. (2010). *The gifts of imperfection: Let go of who you think you're supposed to be and embrace who you are.* Hazelden.

8. Siegel, D. J. (2012). *The developing mind: How relationships and the brain interact to shape who we are.* Guilford Press.

SYNOPSIS OF PART III

THE 10 METHODS OF HEALING YOURSELF (BODY-CENTERED APPROACH)

Part III shifts the focus from *giving it back* to *restoring yourself*—because healing isn't just about releasing emotional burdens, but also about reclaiming wholeness in mind, body, and spirit. This section introduces **The 10 Methods of Healing Yourself**, a body-centered approach designed to help you recognize where trauma is stored and how to release it physically, emotionally, and spiritually.

Many people mistakenly believe healing is only a mental or emotional process. However, research shows that trauma embeds itself in the body, manifesting as chronic pain, muscle tension, digestive issues, and other physical symptoms (Van der Kolk, 2014). The body remembers what the mind tries to forget. That's why *true healing* requires addressing the connection between **trauma, emotions, and the body**. Each chapter in this section explores a specific region of the body where burdens are stored and provides tools for releasing them.

We begin with *Healing the Head & Neck Area*, where tension often accumulates due to overthinking, anxiety, and self-doubt. This chapter teaches how mindfulness, breathwork, and cognitive reframing can alleviate mental strain and restore clarity.

In *Healing the Shoulders & Chest Area*, we explore how grief, responsibility, and unspoken emotions weigh down the upper body. Through heart-opening exercises, deep breathing techniques, and self-compassion practices, we learn to release the pressure of carrying what was never ours.

Healing the Stomach & Diaphragm Area dives into the gut-brain connection, illustrating how trauma impacts digestion, energy levels, and overall well-being. This chapter introduces dietary adjustments, core-strengthening exercises, and breathing techniques to ease stored tension.

Moving downward, *Healing the Pelvis & Hips Area* focuses on past traumas, relationships, and deeply held fears that reside in the body's foundation. Through movement-based therapies, somatic exercises, and grounding techniques, we explore how to regain stability and confidence.

Finally, *Healing the Legs & Feet Area* addresses movement, direction, and the fear of moving forward. Many people feel stuck in life because they are unconsciously holding onto fear in their lower body. This chapter provides tools for physical realignment, stretching, and movement practices that restore a sense of momentum and purpose.

Throughout this section, we integrate **spiritual practices, psychological insights, and physical exercises** to create a **holistic healing approach**. We explore how ancient traditions, modern science, and personal reflection can help release stored trauma and restore **wholeness, peace, and vitality**.

Part III is where we reconnect with our bodies, ensuring that as we give back the burdens that don't belong to us, we also **heal, rebuild, and move forward** with strength and resilience. This is the path to lasting transformation—where freedom is not just a concept, but an embodied experience.

CHAPTER 6

PICK UP THE RUG

M any of us have spent years sweeping things under the rug—pushing down emotions, ignoring past hurts, and hoping that what we refuse to face will eventually disappear. But the truth is, what we suppress, accumulates. It does not simply go away. Trauma, emotional burdens, and unspoken pain settle into the very fabric of our being, affecting not just our spirit and soul but also our physical bodies.

When we refuse to deal with what's under the rug, we carry it in our mind, our emotions, and our physical bodies. Anxiety, depression, chronic stress, and even physical ailments can stem from unresolved trauma (Van der Kolk, 2014). The body keeps the score, and our healing begins when we are brave enough to **pick up the rug**—to look at what's been swept beneath. Then after we take a look at it, we've got to shake it out, and roll it up for good.

The Weight of What's Unspoken

The rug is a metaphor for our **spirit, soul, and body**. It's where all the hidden things go—the secrets we've kept, the traumas we've endured, and the emotional projections we've absorbed from others. And just like an actual rug, when we lift it, we might find dust, dirt, and debris that have been there for years. **But ignoring it won't make it go away.**

Jesus said in Luke 8:17, *"For nothing is hidden that will not be made manifest, nor is anything secret that will not be known and come to light."* Healing requires confrontation. We cannot heal what we refuse to acknowledge. Picking up the rug means confronting the past, recognizing what has been stored inside us, and choosing to deal with it instead of burying it deeper.

My Wake-Up Call: When My Body Screamed at Me

I didn't fully understand how unresolved trauma lived inside my body until life forced me to. The day after Thanksgiving 2021, my wife, kids, and I were in a serious car accident up the street from our home. This would be the first of two major accidents my family was in. The latter would be with my mother included in Summer of 2023. What seemed like a manageable situation at first soon unraveled into something that shook me to my core.

In the months following the first accident, my body began to break down in ways I never imagined. Sciatica and pelvic pain made even the simplest movements excruciating. The idea of sitting or standing was unbearable. Lower back pain made it nearly impossible to get out of bed—at times, my wife had to physically lift me to help me stand. Some days, I could barely walk at all. At just thirty-one and thirty-two years old, I felt like I was losing my ability to move, and it sent me into a deep depression. On the outside, I had what everyone wanted: a beautiful home that was five-thousand square feet of space with a three-car garage, a beautiful and brilliant wife, two amazing kids, a great career in healthcare management, making phenomenal money, leading a church community as Lead Pastor, travelling to go on trips almost every month. I mean, on the outside, I had *"the life."* But there were things brewing on the inside of me that these accidents would serve as a metaphorical wake-up for.

When the physical pain persisted, I turned to doctors, chiropractic services, and other medical interventions, hoping for relief. And when that didn't work, I desperately turned to God and those who I considered His servants that had the healing touch. But no matter what treatments or prayers I pursued, nothing seemed to work. Instead, things got worse. I began experiencing chest pains and anxiety attacks so severe that I thought I was having heart attacks and strokes. The external stressors in my life—like some of the relationships I had and the expectations that certain communities I was apart of placed on me—only exacerbated the issue, leading me to develop adult-onset asthma. My body was crying out for me to listen. When I finally felt the pain of it all, I ran to the doctors only for them to not have a clue of how to heal me. Everything else I was experiencing was not from the accident. So where was it all coming from? And why all of a sudden now when I crossed over into my thirties? Aren't my early thirties supposed to be the prime years of my life? This state of the unknown almost drove me crazy...and my wife too. *Ha!* God bless her. She was the one that had to listen to all of my bickering, crying, whining, and complaining for years as I dealt with this behind closed doors. Without knowing it, I had begun to do to her what others had did to me for so long, which was why I ended up in that state in the first place. I didn't know it then, but I begin to trauma-dump on her. I begin to expect her to save me. In my head, I put her in a position of playing my Savior. And let me tell you—after four years of this—that did not end up well. She had her own traumas to deal with. But I was desperate. I needed relief and I had the slightest clue what was happening to me back then. The most challenging part was that, during this time, I could pray for everyone else and see them walk in their healing; but I could not pray myself into my own healing.

It took time for me to realize the truth: **I was not sick—I was traumatized. My body had become the storage unit for decades of stress, pain, and unresolved emotional wounds.** The accident had been the catalyst, but the roots of my suffering had been buried long before that moment. And I knew that if I wanted to heal, I had to do more than just treat symptoms—I had to deal with the trauma itself.

Dealing with What's Under the Rug

When trauma isn't addressed, it settles into the body like dust settles into the fabric of a rug. Research confirms that stored trauma can lead to chronic pain, autoimmune issues, digestive problems, and nervous system dysregulation (Gabor, 2021). Just as dust and dirt collect under a rug, trauma accumulates in our muscles, joints, and nervous system.

Picking up the rug means dealing with both the emotional and the physical. Here's how it should go:

1. **Lift the rug (Confront the secrets)** – Acknowledge the trauma, memories, and emotions we have tried to suppress.

2. **Shake out the rug (Release projections and false burdens)** – Recognize what was never ours to carry and intentionally giving it back.

3. **Roll up the rug (Let go of trauma stored in the body)** – Engage in healing practices that address both mind and body.

Practical Ways to "Shake Out the Rug" and Release Trauma

1. **Somatic Healing Practices**

   o Trauma lives in the nervous system. Engaging in **gentle movement, stretching, and body-based therapies** can help the body process stored trauma (Levine, 2010). Deep breathing, palates, exercises and massage therapy can be powerful tools for release.

2. **Emotional Processing Through Writing and Therapy**

   o Keeping things bottled up only reinforces trauma. Journaling, therapy, and talking through past experiences help to bring healing. Studies show that **expressive writing reduces stress** and improves emotional resilience (Pennebaker, 1997).

3. **Spiritual Alignment and Trusting God for Healing**

   o The mind and body cannot heal without the soul. **Faith, prayer, and trust in divine healing create the space for full restoration.** *Psalm 147:3 reminds us: "He heals the brokenhearted and binds up their wounds."*

4. **Breathwork and Mindfulness to Regulate the Nervous System**

   o Intentional breathing helps reset the body's response to trauma. **Deep belly breathing** and **progressive relaxation techniques** can calm the nervous system, reducing anxiety and stress (Kabat-Zinn, 1990).

Rolling Up the Rug: Giving Trauma Back and Reclaiming Your Health

After you've done the work to identify and release, then there comes a moment when you must **roll up the rug and remove it completely.** The things that once lived under it—the generational traumas, the projections, the unspoken pains—no longer have to define you. My journey to healing taught me that **the body has an incredible ability to heal when we stop suppressing and start surrendering.** When we start letting go of what's not ours.

Picking up the rug is an act of courage. It is choosing to face what has been hidden, release what was never ours, and reclaim what rightfully belongs to us—our health, peace, and freedom.

So, I ask you: What have you been sweeping under the rug? And are you ready to pick it up, shake it out, and roll it away for good? In the next few chapters we're going to hyper focus on healing the body, by identifying what's been hiding underneath the surface.

FOOTNOTES

1. Van der Kolk, B. (2014). *The body keeps the score: Brain, mind, and body in the healing of trauma.* Penguin Publishing Group.

2. Gabor, M. (2021). *The myth of normal: Trauma, illness, and healing in a toxic culture.* Avery Publishing.

3. Levine, P. A. (2010). *In an unspoken voice: How the body releases trauma and restores goodness.* North Atlantic Books.

4. Pennebaker, J. W. (1997). *Opening up: The healing power of expressing emotions.* Guilford Press.

5. Kabat-Zinn, J. (1990). *Full catastrophe living: Using the wisdom of your body and mind to face stress, pain, and illness.* Delacorte.

SYNOPSIS OF PART III

THE 10 METHODS OF HEALING YOURSELF (BODY-CENTERED APPROACH)

Part III shifts the focus from giving burdens back to rebuilding and restoring ourselves. This section explores the body-centered approach to healing, demonstrating how emotional pain is stored in different areas of the body and providing targeted methods for releasing it.

Each chapter in this section focuses on a specific body region, breaking down the physical, emotional, and spiritual aspects of stored trauma:

1. Healing the Head & Neck – Addressing mental overactivity, self-doubt, and tension headaches through cognitive reframing and relaxation techniques.

2. Healing the Shoulders & Chest – Releasing feelings of obligation, responsibility, and grief that weigh heavily on the upper body.

3. Healing the Stomach & Diaphragm – Exploring the gut-brain connection, anxiety storage, and breathwork techniques for nervous system regulation.

4. Healing the Pelvis & Hips – Addressing trauma linked to relationships, security, and personal stability through movement-based therapy.

5. Healing the Legs & Feet – Overcoming fear of moving forward by re-establishing physical and spiritual grounding.

By integrating breathwork, movement, prayer, and mindfulness, this section teaches readers how to release physical manifestations of emotional pain. *The 10 Methods of Healing Yourself* ensure that as we let go of false burdens, we actively heal the parts of ourselves that were affected by them.

CHAPTER 7

HEALING THE HEAD & NECK AREA

The head and neck are often the first places where stress, anxiety, and emotional burdens manifest physically. Headaches, migraines, neck stiffness, and chronic tension can all be indicators that **the mental load you are carrying is too heavy**. When we internalize worries, overthink situations, or replay past traumas in our minds, the body reacts by tightening muscles and restricting blood flow, leading to physical discomfort (Van der Kolk, 2014). Healing the head and neck area requires a combination of **mental release, spiritual renewal, and physical realignment**.

The Mind-Body Connection: Why We Carry Stress in the Head and Neck

Negative thoughts don't just stay in the mind—they create tension throughout the body. The **head** represents thoughts, perceptions, and intellectual processing, while the **neck** connects the head to the body, symbolizing flexibility, communication, and the ability to look forward in life. When we feel mentally stuck, indecisive, or burdened by thoughts that aren't ours to carry, the body responds by tightening the neck and shoulders (Sapolsky, 2004).

Common symptoms of stress in the head and neck area include:

- Frequent headaches or migraines

- Tightness in the jaw (often linked to suppressed emotions or unspoken words)

- Stiff neck and upper shoulders

- Feeling mentally "foggy" or overwhelmed

- Difficulty concentrating due to racing thoughts

Releasing Mental Chatter: The Power of Thought Detoxing

Romans 12:2 reminds us: *"Do not be conformed to this world, but be transformed by the renewing of your mind."* Renewal begins with recognizing and **releasing mental chatter**—the internal dialogue that fuels stress and anxiety. If you constantly replay conversations, worry about things beyond your control, or struggle with self-doubt, your mind is likely overcrowded.

A **thought detox** is a practice of releasing unhealthy mental loops. Here are three ways to clear the clutter:

1. **Journaling for Clarity** – Writing down intrusive thoughts helps externalize worries, making them easier to process. Try a 5-minute **brain dump** where you write

without judgment until your mind feels lighter (Pennebaker, 1997).

2. **Spoken Affirmations** – Speak life over your mind. Replace thoughts of fear and worry with declarations like:

   o *"My mind is clear, my body is at ease."*

   o *"I release thoughts that do not serve me."*

   o *"I trust God to renew my mind and give me peace."*

3. **Mindful Awareness** – Throughout the day, pause and ask: *"Is this thought true? Does it belong to me? Can I release it?"* Learning to distinguish between **your thoughts** and **projected anxieties** from others helps prevent mental exhaustion.

Physical Exercises: Releasing Tension in the Head and Neck

Since the mind and body are deeply connected, physical exercises can help **release mental burdens**. When you experience tension headaches or neck stiffness, try these techniques:

1. **Neck Stretches**

   o Sit tall, drop your right ear toward your right shoulder, and hold for 20 seconds.

   o Slowly roll your chin down toward your chest, then over to the left shoulder.

   o Repeat 3 times to release tightness.

2. **Deep Breathing for Mental Release**

   o Inhale deeply through your nose for 4 seconds, hold for 4 seconds, then exhale slowly for 6 seconds.

   o Repeat this cycle 5-10 times, imagining stress melting away with each breath.

3. **Guided Meditation on Letting Go**

   o Close your eyes and visualize a soft golden light surrounding your head and neck.

   o As you inhale, say: *"I breathe in clarity."*

   o As you exhale, say: *"I release mental burdens."*

   o Continue for 5 minutes, allowing the tension to dissolve.

Spiritual Renewal: Releasing Thoughts That Don't Serve You

When **mental clutter** builds up, it prevents us from hearing divine wisdom and trusting in God's plan. Proverbs 3:5-6 instructs us to *"Trust in the Lord with all your heart and lean not on your own understanding."* Too often, we hold onto unnecessary worries, forgetting that **faith and surrender create peace**.

A simple spiritual practice to align with **mental renewal**:

- **Pray over your thoughts**: Ask God to remove false burdens and replace them with divine peace.

- **Fast from negativity**: Limit exposure to stressful media, toxic conversations, or anything that fuels mental chaos.

- **Surround yourself with wisdom**: Read scripture, listen to uplifting messages, and engage with people who encourage mental and spiritual clarity.

Moving Forward: Daily Practices for a Clear Mind and a Relaxed Body

Healing the head and neck area isn't a one-time event—it's a **daily practice**. Here are ways to maintain mental and physical clarity:

- **Morning ritual:** Start the day with prayer, affirmations, or journaling.

- **Midday check-in:** Notice any tension in your head or neck and do a quick breathwork reset.

- **Evening reflection:** Before bed, release worries through meditation or scripture reading.

By consistently practicing these techniques, you will begin to notice a **lighter mind, relaxed body, and greater spiritual clarity**. The goal is not just to remove tension, but to replace it with **peace, wisdom, and resilience**.

FOOTNOTES

1. Van der Kolk, B. (2014). *The body keeps the score: Brain, mind, and body in the healing of trauma.* Penguin Publishing Group.

2. Sapolsky, R. M. (2004). *Why zebras don't get ulcers: The acclaimed guide to stress, stress-related diseases, and coping.* Holt Paperbacks.

3. Pennebaker, J. W. (1997). *Opening up: The healing power of expressing emotions.* Guilford Press.

CHAPTER 8

HEALING THE SHOULDERS & CHEST AREA

Our shoulders and chest often bear the physical manifestations of **stress, anxiety, and unprocessed emotions**. Many of us unconsciously tense our shoulders, hunch forward, or experience tightness in the chest without realizing that these are signs of emotional weight being carried in the body. The phrase **"carrying the weight of the world on your shoulders"** is not just a metaphor—it is a physiological and psychological reality.

Understanding the connection between **stress and the upper body** is crucial for healing. When we store burdens—whether personal worries, family responsibilities, or societal expectations—we unconsciously tighten our **shoulders and chest**. This tension can lead to chronic pain, reduced lung capacity, and even a sense of emotional suffocation.

By learning to **release these burdens physically, emotionally, and spiritually**, we allow ourselves to breathe freely, stand tall, and walk lighter.

The Mind-Body Connection: How Stress Affects the Shoulders & Chest

When we experience stress or trauma, the **body's nervous system** activates its fight-or-flight response, causing muscles in the shoulders to tighten and breathing to become shallow (Sapolsky, 2004). Over time, this tension becomes chronic, leading to:

- **Stiffness and pain in the shoulders and upper back**

- **Shallow breathing and tightness in the chest**

- **Poor posture, leading to further discomfort and fatigue**

- **Anxiety-related symptoms, including panic attacks**

- **Emotional suppression, as the chest area is associated with the heart and expression of emotions**

Proverbs 12:25 tells us, *"Anxiety in a man's heart weighs him down, but a good word makes him glad."* The literal weight we feel in our shoulders is often an external manifestation of **internalized burdens**. To heal, we must address both the physical and emotional dimensions.

Practical Exercise: Heart-Opening Stretches & Mindful Breathing

Releasing tension in the shoulders and chest requires a combination of movement and intentional breathing. Here are some simple yet effective techniques:

1. Shoulder Roll & Release

- Sit or stand with your back straight.

- Inhale deeply as you lift your shoulders toward your ears.

- Exhale slowly as you roll your shoulders backward and downward.

- Repeat 5 times to loosen tension.

2. Heart-Opening Stretch

- Stand tall and clasp your hands behind your back.

- Straighten your arms and lift your chest toward the ceiling.

- Hold for 15–20 seconds, breathing deeply.

- Release and repeat twice.

3. Deep Chest Breathing for Anxiety Relief

- Sit comfortably and place one hand on your heart and the other on your abdomen.

- Inhale slowly through your nose, allowing your chest to expand.

- Exhale through your mouth, releasing tension with each breath.

- Repeat for 5 minutes, focusing on **letting go** of emotional weight.

Studies show that **deep breathing activates the parasympathetic nervous system, reducing stress and promoting relaxation** (Kabat-Zinn, 1990). By practicing these movements and breathwork daily, we begin to **rewire the body's stress response**, making space for peace.

Spiritual Exercise: Letting Burdens Roll Off Your Shoulders

Just as our shoulders physically carry stress, our **spirit carries emotional and mental burdens**. Many of us hold onto responsibilities that were never meant for us to carry alone. **Matthew 11:28-30** reminds us of Jesus' invitation: *"Come to me, all who labor and are heavy laden, and I will give you rest."*

To practice this surrender, try this **visualization exercise:**

1. **Find a quiet place** where you can sit comfortably.

2. **Close your eyes** and take a deep breath.

3. **Visualize your burdens**—imagine each stressor as a physical weight on your shoulders.

4. **Imagine Jesus standing before you, extending His hands.**

5. As you exhale, **picture yourself lifting these burdens off your shoulders and placing them into His hands.**

6. Breathe in peace, **feeling your shoulders relax** and your chest expand with freedom.

7. **Repeat until you feel lighter.**

This spiritual practice is a **reminder that we are not alone in our struggles.** We are called to **release, not retain**—to give back what was never meant for us to carry.

Emotional Healing: Releasing Suppressed Feelings

The chest is home to the heart, where emotions such as grief, love, and joy reside. When we suppress emotions, we create blockages in our ability to express ourselves fully. Research shows that **emotional suppression is linked to increased stress, higher blood pressure, and overall poorer health outcomes** (Gross & Levenson, 1997).

Ways to Emotionally Release Suppressed Feelings:

1. **Journaling:** Write about what burdens your heart, without judgment.

2. **Speaking Your Truth:** Have a conversation with someone you trust, or express your emotions out loud in a safe space.

3. **Crying:** Tears are a natural release mechanism—allow yourself to grieve and let go.

4. **Laughter Therapy:** Engage in activities that bring genuine joy to lighten the emotional weight in your chest.

Moving Forward: Daily Practices for a Lighter Heart

To keep your **shoulders light and chest open**, incorporate these habits into your daily routine:

- **Morning Check-In:** Take a moment to stretch and breathe before starting your day.

- **Midday Reset:** Perform a quick shoulder roll and deep breathing exercise if tension arises.

- **Evening Reflection:** Before bed, mentally and spiritually release any burdens accumulated throughout the day.

By **practicing physical movement, emotional expression, and spiritual surrender,** we create space for **freedom, joy, and healing**. Healing isn't about forcing pain away—it's about gently **letting go** and allowing the body, mind, and spirit to rest.

FOOTNOTES

1. Sapolsky, R. M. (2004). *Why zebras don't get ulcers: The acclaimed guide to stress, stress-related diseases, and coping.* Holt Paperbacks.

2. Kabat-Zinn, J. (1990). *Full catastrophe living: Using the wisdom of your body and mind to face stress, pain, and illness.* Delacorte.

3. Gross, J. J., & Levenson, R. W. (1997). Emotional suppression: Physiology, self-report, and expressive behavior. *Journal of Personality and Social Psychology, 72*(3), 435-448.

CHAPTER 9

HEALING THE STOMACH & DIAPHRAGM AREA

The stomach and diaphragm area is often referred to as the body's **emotional center**, closely linked to **gut feelings, fear, worry, and shame**. Have you ever felt "butterflies" before a big moment, a sinking feeling in your stomach after bad news, or nausea from anxiety? These sensations are not just in your head—science confirms that the **gut and brain are deeply connected** through the **gut-brain axis**, which plays a crucial role in emotional regulation, stress response, and overall well-being (Mayer, 2011).

When trauma, stress, or prolonged anxiety is left unprocessed, it often manifests in **digestive issues, bloating, acid reflux, irritable bowel syndrome (IBS), and breathing difficulties** due to diaphragm tightness. Healing this area requires **a combination of physiological, psychological, and spiritual interventions** to release stored emotions and restore balance to the nervous system.

The Science: The Gut-Brain Axis & The Vagus Nerve

The **gut-brain axis** is the bidirectional communication system between the **gut and the brain**, primarily regulated by the **vagus nerve**, the longest cranial nerve in the body. This system allows the brain to send signals to the gut and vice versa, meaning that **stress, trauma, and anxiety can directly impact digestion and stomach function** (Cryan & Dinan, 2012).

How Stress Affects the Stomach & Diaphragm:

- **Activates the "fight-or-flight" response**, reducing blood flow to the digestive system, leading to bloating, nausea, or stomach cramps.

- **Increases cortisol levels**, disrupting the gut's microbiome and contributing to inflammation (Chrousos, 2009).

- **Tightens the diaphragm**, restricting deep breathing and reinforcing stress patterns in the nervous system.

By calming the nervous system, particularly through diaphragmatic breathing and vagus nerve activation, we can **restore gut health, ease digestive issues, and release stored emotional stress.**

Practical Exercise: Diaphragmatic Breathing to Calm the Nervous System

Diaphragmatic breathing, also known as belly breathing, is a proven method for **activating the vagus nerve, reducing stress hormones, and restoring balance to the gut and**

diaphragm area (Porges, 2011). This technique signals to the body that it is safe, shifting the nervous system from a **fight-or-flight state to a rest-and-digest mode.**

How to Practice Diaphragmatic Breathing:

1. **Find a comfortable seated or lying-down position.** Place one hand on your chest and the other on your belly.

2. **Inhale deeply through your nose, allowing your belly to rise while keeping your chest still.**

3. **Exhale slowly through your mouth, feeling your belly fall.**

4. **Repeat this process for 5-10 minutes, focusing on relaxing your stomach and diaphragm.**

5. As you breathe, internally affirm: *"I am safe. I release fear. I embrace peace."*

Studies show that **consistent practice of diaphragmatic breathing can lower anxiety, reduce inflammation, and improve gut function** (Jerath et al., 2006). Making this a daily habit will help heal both emotional and physical tension in the stomach area.

Spiritual Exercise: Casting Cares & Releasing Worry

In **1 Peter 5:7**, we are reminded: *"Cast all your anxiety on Him because He cares for you."* Worry and fear are some of the heaviest burdens we carry, often **settling deep into the stomach** as tightness, discomfort, or digestive issues. Just as we can physically release tension through breathwork, we must also spiritually release emotional burdens by surrendering them to God.

Visualization Exercise: Letting Go of Burdens

1. **Find a quiet space** where you won't be disturbed.

2. **Close your eyes and take a deep breath.**

3. **Picture yourself standing by a river, holding a stone that represents your fears, worries, or past traumas.**

4. **As you exhale, visualize yourself throwing the stone into the water, watching the ripples carry it away.**

5. **Affirm to yourself:**

   o *"I release fear and embrace trust."*

   o *"I let go of what no longer serves me."*

   o *"I cast my cares on God, knowing that He holds my future."*

6. **Breathe deeply, feeling the weight lift from your body.**

Letting go isn't just a one-time act—it's a **daily practice of surrendering stress, choosing peace, and trusting that you are supported.**

The Connection Between Trauma and Digestion

Unprocessed trauma affects digestion and gut health. Many people with chronic stomach issues have a history of **stress, anxiety, or past emotional wounds** (Dinan & Cryan, 2017). Healing requires a holistic approach—addressing both the **physical and emotional** layers of stored trauma.

Steps to Restore Gut Health and Emotional Balance:

1. **Eat mindfully** – Avoid processed foods and excessive caffeine, which can heighten gut sensitivity.

2. **Engage in breathwork and gentle movement** – Yoga, stretching, and deep breathing can regulate the gut-brain connection.

3. **Process emotions regularly** – Journaling, therapy, or talking with a trusted friend can help prevent emotional buildup.

4. **Prioritize spiritual alignment** – Meditate on scriptures about peace, release worries through prayer, and lean into God's strength.

Moving Forward: Listening to Your Body's Messages

The **stomach and diaphragm are deeply connected to our sense of security, peace, and emotional stability.** When something feels off in your gut, **it's often your body's way of signaling unresolved stress or emotional weight.**

Ask yourself daily:

- *What emotions am I holding in my stomach?*

- *What fears do I need to release?*

- *Have I taken time to breathe deeply and reset my nervous system today?*

By practicing **diaphragmatic breathing, releasing worry, and nurturing both the body and spirit**, we can restore balance, reclaim peace, and truly begin the process of **healing from within.**

FOOTNOTES

1. Mayer, E. A. (2011). Gut feelings: The emerging biology of gut-brain communication. *Nature Reviews Neuroscience,* 12(8), 453-466.

2. Cryan, J. F., & Dinan, T. G. (2012). Mind-altering microorganisms: The impact of the gut microbiota on brain and behavior. *Nature Reviews Neuroscience,* 13(10), 701-712.

3. Chrousos, G. P. (2009). Stress and disorders of the stress system. *Nature Reviews Endocrinology,* 5(7), 374-381.

4. Porges, S. W. (2011). *The polyvagal theory: Neurophysiological foundations of emotions, attachment, communication, and self-regulation.* W.W. Norton & Company.

5. Jerath, R., Edry, J. W., Barnes, V. A., & Jerath, V. (2006). Physiology of long pranayamic breathing: Neural respiratory elements may provide a mechanism that explains how slow deep breathing shifts the autonomic nervous system. *Medical Hypotheses,* 67(3), 566-571.

6. Dinan, T. G., & Cryan, J. F. (2017). The microbiome-gut-brain axis in health and disease. *Gastroenterology Clinics of North America,* 46(1), 77-89.

CHAPTER 10

HEALING THE PELVIS & HIPS AREA

T he **pelvis and hips** serve as the foundation of our body's stability and movement, but they are also known to store deep-seated **emotional tension, past trauma, and unresolved relationship wounds.** Many people carry stress, fear, or pain in their hips without realizing that the tension is not just physical—it is often tied to **security, relationships, and stored emotions** (Levine, 2010).

From a physiological perspective, the hips are home to **major muscle groups,** including the **psoas** (often called the "muscle of the soul"), which connects the upper and lower body. Research suggests that **chronic tension in the psoas can be linked to past trauma and emotional suppression,** particularly around themes of **safety, intimacy, and control** (Van der Kolk, 2014). If you have ever felt stuck in life or unable to move forward after a difficult experience, your body may be holding onto **that emotional residue in the hips.**

By engaging in **intentional movement, breathwork, and spiritual release**, we can begin the process of unlocking emotional and physical freedom in this part of the body.

The Science: Trauma and Emotional Storage in the Hips

When we experience **stress or trauma**, the body responds by tightening muscles as a **protective mechanism**. This response often manifests in the hips, where the **fight-or-flight response** can remain activated long after a traumatic event has passed (Porges, 2011).

Common symptoms of emotional tension stored in the pelvis and hips:

- **Tight hip flexors or limited mobility**
- **Lower back pain or discomfort**
- **Feelings of heaviness in the pelvic region**
- **Difficulties with intimacy or trust**
- **A sense of being stuck or unable to move forward emotionally**

Understanding that the **body holds onto past experiences** allows us to work through emotional pain in a more holistic way, using both **physical movement and emotional release techniques**.

Practical Exercise: Hip-Openers & Walking Meditations

Movement is one of the most powerful ways to release stored trauma. Since the hips and pelvis are heavily involved in **stability and forward motion**, incorporating intentional **hip-opening exercises and walking meditations** can help create a sense of release and flow.

1. Hip-Opening Stretches

Practicing **gentle hip stretches** helps to release tightness and stored emotional energy. Try these simple exercises:

- **Seated Butterfly Stretch**: Sit on the floor, bring the soles of your feet together, and let your knees drop outward. Hold for 30 seconds while breathing deeply.

- **Pigeon Pose**: Bring one leg forward, keeping the other extended behind you. Fold forward slightly and hold for 20–30 seconds on each side.

- **Lunging Hip Stretch**: Step one foot forward into a deep lunge, pressing your hips forward while keeping your back leg extended. Hold for 20 seconds per side.

2. Walking Meditation to Move Energy

- **Find a quiet path or space to walk.**

- **With each step, focus on an intention—whether it's releasing past pain, forgiving someone, or opening yourself to new experiences.**

- As you exhale, visualize stored tension dissolving from your hips and pelvis.

- Walk for at least 10 minutes, staying mindful of each movement.

Studies show that **conscious walking helps regulate the nervous system and increase emotional resilience** (Kabat-Zinn, 1990). Moving with **intention** allows stored emotions to **shift and release**, preventing stagnation.

Spiritual Reflection: Letting Go of Unresolved Relationship Wounds

The **pelvic region is associated with relationships, intimacy, and security**. Whether it's childhood attachment wounds, romantic betrayals, or familial disappointments, unresolved relational pain often **settles in the hips and lower body**.

Psalm 55:22 reminds us: *"Cast your burden on the Lord, and He will sustain you."* Holding onto pain from the past does not protect us—it only keeps us weighed down. Healing requires a conscious decision to **release what is no longer serving us**.

Guided Reflection: Releasing Relationship Wounds

1. **Find a quiet space where you feel safe.**

2. **Close your eyes and take a deep breath.**

3. **Bring to mind any past relationship wounds— hurtful words, betrayals, disappointments.**

4. **Imagine holding those wounds in your hands, acknowledging them without judgment.**

5. **Now, visualize placing them into God's hands, one by one.**

6. **As you release them, affirm:**

   o *"I let go of past pain and open myself to healing."*

   o *"I am safe. I am whole. I am free."*

7. **Breathe deeply and feel your hips softening as the weight lifts.**

This practice, done consistently, allows for deep emotional and spiritual renewal. **Forgiveness and release do not mean forgetting, but rather, choosing to no longer carry the burden.**

Moving Forward: Restoring Stability and Emotional Freedom

Healing the pelvis and hips is about more than physical flexibility—it's about **emotional and spiritual mobility.** If you've felt stuck, uncertain, or disconnected, your body may be asking you to release what has been **stored in silence.**

Daily Practices for Continued Healing:

- **Engage in daily hip-opening stretches** to maintain flexibility.

- **Walk with intention,** setting healing-focused goals.

- **Practice forgiveness** and release past pain through prayer and journaling.

- **Trust that your body is always communicating with you—listen to its signals.**

By consistently tending to this area of the body, you will begin to notice **greater ease, confidence, and emotional resilience.** Healing is not about erasing the past but **creating space for new growth and freedom.**

So, as you continue this journey, ask yourself: **What am I ready to let go of?** And when the answer comes, take a deep breath, **step forward, and release it.**

FOOTNOTES

1. Levine, P. A. (2010). *In an unspoken voice: How the body releases trauma and restores goodness.* North Atlantic Books.

2. Van der Kolk, B. (2014). *The body keeps the score: Brain, mind, and body in the healing of trauma.* Penguin Publishing Group.

3. Porges, S. W. (2011). *The polyvagal theory: Neurophysiological foundations of emotions, attachment, communication, and self-regulation.* W.W. Norton & Company.

4. Kabat-Zinn, J. (1990). *Full catastrophe living: Using the wisdom of your body and mind to face stress, pain, and illness.* Delacorte.

CHAPTER 11

HEALING THE LEG & FEET AREA

Our **legs and feet** are not just responsible for movement; they are symbolic of **stability, direction, and progress**. When emotional burdens, fears, and anxieties weigh us down, our legs and feet can bear the consequences. Many people experience **restless legs, foot pain, or chronic tightness** in their lower body, unaware that these sensations may be rooted in **emotional and spiritual struggles**.

If the **head represents thought and the shoulders carry stress, then the legs and feet represent movement**—our ability to step forward into the future with confidence and purpose. When trauma, anxiety, or uncertainty grips us, it can manifest as **hesitation, lack of stability, and even physical pain in our legs and feet** (Van der Kolk, 2014).

Healing this area requires a combination of **physical grounding, emotional release, and spiritual reinforcement**, allowing us to regain balance and walk boldly in our divine purpose.

The Mind-Body Connection: Anxiety, Restlessness & Leg Tension

Scientific research has shown that **stress and anxiety can directly impact the lower body,** often leading to conditions such as **restless leg syndrome (RLS), chronic leg tension, and foot pain** (Walters et al., 2018). When the nervous system is overactive, **blood flow to the legs can be disrupted,** causing discomfort and an inability to fully relax.

Common symptoms of stored emotional tension in the legs and feet:

- **Restless leg syndrome (RLS)** – Uncontrollable leg movements, often triggered by stress and nervous system overactivity.

- **Chronic foot pain or tension** – A sensation of tightness or heaviness in the feet due to emotional stagnation.

- **Feeling "stuck" in life** – Difficulty making decisions, moving forward, or stepping into new opportunities.

- **Weakness or instability** – A lack of confidence in one's personal path, often mirroring spiritual or emotional uncertainty.

When we understand how **emotional blocks can disrupt physical movement,** we can begin the work of restoring **freedom, stability, and direction** in our lives.

Practical Exercise: Grounding Techniques for Stability

To **heal the legs and feet,** we must **reconnect with the earth,** reestablishing a sense of security and movement. **Grounding techniques** help restore physical and emotional balance by **calming the nervous system and enhancing body awareness** (Porges, 2011).

1. Barefoot Walking for Emotional Grounding

Walking barefoot on natural surfaces such as **grass, sand, or soil** is a proven grounding technique that **reduces inflammation, improves circulation, and calms the nervous system** (Chevalier et al., 2012).

How to practice barefoot grounding:

- Find a natural surface (grass, dirt, or sand) and **walk slowly for 5-10 minutes.**

- As you walk, **focus on each step,** feeling the **connection between your feet and the earth.**

- Breathe deeply, allowing any tension in your legs to **release into the ground.**

- Imagine stress **draining out through your feet,** leaving you feeling more stable and secure.

2. Foot Massage to Release Stored Tension

Massaging the feet is an effective way to **stimulate circulation, release emotional stress, and ease physical tightness.**

How to perform a self-foot massage:

- Sit in a comfortable position and **apply firm pressure to the soles of your feet.**

- Use your thumbs to press into **tight spots**, holding for 10 seconds before releasing.

- Focus on areas that feel tense, **breathing deeply** with each movement.

- As you massage, repeat affirmations like **"I release all tension. I am grounded and steady."**

Regular foot massages **improve mobility, reduce stress-related tension, and reconnect us with our physical foundation.**

Spiritual Principle: Standing Firm in Faith & Purpose

The **Bible frequently references the importance of standing firm in faith**, a principle that parallels the importance of **physical and emotional grounding**.

1 Corinthians 16:13 tells us: *"Be on your guard; stand firm in the faith; be courageous; be strong."* Just as we must **strengthen our legs to stand physically**, we must also **strengthen our faith to stand spiritually.**

Spiritual Exercise: Visualization & Prayer for Stability

1. Find a quiet place where you can stand barefoot or sit with your feet on the floor.

2. Close your eyes and take a deep breath.

3. Imagine roots growing from the soles of your feet, deeply anchoring you into God's presence.

4. As you inhale, say: *"I am firmly planted in faith."*

5. As you exhale, release fear, doubt, and instability.

6. Repeat this for several minutes, focusing on the sensation of being grounded, both physically and spiritually.

This exercise reinforces that **our foundation is unshakable when rooted in faith.** We may face trials, but we are not easily moved when we stand firm in God's promises.

Moving Forward: Daily Practices for Strength and Stability

To maintain healing in the legs and feet, commit to daily practices that encourage movement, release tension, and reinforce spiritual stability.

1. **Daily Grounding Walks:** Spend time each day walking barefoot or connecting intentionally with the ground.

2. **Leg & Foot Stretches:** Incorporate stretches that promote flexibility and circulation in the lower body.

3. **Faith-Based Affirmations:** Speak truths over yourself, such as:

   o *"I stand firm in my faith and purpose."*

   o *"I am moving forward in confidence."*

   o *"My foundation is strong, and I walk in freedom."*

4. **Prayer & Meditation:** Spend time in reflection, casting your worries onto God and reaffirming your direction.

By integrating these habits, you **restore balance, stability, and movement**—both physically and spiritually. Healing is about **taking the next step forward**, trusting that you are supported on every level.

So, as you walk this journey, ask yourself: **What is holding me back from stepping forward?** And when the answer comes, take a deep breath, **stand firm, and move boldly.**

FOOTNOTES

1. Walters, A. S., Ondo, W. G., & Zhu, W. (2018). Restless legs syndrome: Theoretical mechanisms, current treatments, and future directions. *Sleep Medicine Reviews*, 42, 1-11.

2. Van der Kolk, B. (2014). *The body keeps the score: Brain, mind, and body in the healing of trauma.* Penguin Publishing Group.

3. Porges, S. W. (2011). *The polyvagal theory: Neurophysiological foundations of emotions, attachment, communication, and self-regulation.* W.W. Norton & Company.

4. Chevalier, G., Sinatra, S. T., Oschman, J. L., Sokal, K., & Sokal, P. (2012). Earthing: Health implications of reconnecting the human body to the Earth's surface electrons. *Journal of Environmental and Public Health*, 2012, 1-8.

SYNOPSIS OF PART IV

LIVING THE 'GIVE IT BACK' LIFESTYLE

Part IV serves as the final integration, helping readers maintain their healing, apply this theory to real life, and extend it to their communities. It's about making *The Give It Back Theory* a lifelong practice rather than a temporary exercise.

Chapter 12: Daily Practices and Maintenance emphasizes the importance of routine emotional hygiene, much like we care for our physical bodies. It revisits the 8 Ways of Giving It Back and the 10 Methods of Healing Yourself, showing readers how to integrate them into their daily lives.

Chapter 13: Real-Life 'Give It Back' Stories & Testimonials showcases personal transformations, illustrating how people from all walks of life have used these principles to overcome burnout, generational trauma, abandonment, and false expectations.

Chapter 14: Your Ongoing Journey—A Call to Action is the book's final challenge and invitation. Using David's story of returning Saul's armor (1 Samuel 17:38-40) and the spiritual law of giving and receiving (Luke 6:38), this chapter encourages readers to embrace their unique calling and walk unburdened by what was never theirs. It calls for bold action, urging readers to pass this message forward by sharing their testimony, joining the movement, and committing to their healing.

Part IV is the culmination of everything The Give It Back Theory stands for—not just relief, but transformation. It reinforces that freedom is available to everyone willing to release what no longer serves them and step into the life they were always meant to live.

CHAPTER 12

DAILY PRACTICES AND
MAINTENANCE

I can't stress this enough. Healing is not a one-time event; it is an ongoing process that requires **daily attention, intention, and action**. Just as we maintain our physical health through nutrition, movement, and rest, our emotional and spiritual well-being needs consistent nurturing. **The work of *giving back* burdens and healing the body requires routine check-ins, self-awareness, and continuous implementation of the tools we've learned.**

To fully embrace daily healing, it's essential to understand how *The 8 Ways of Giving It Back* complement *The 10 Methods of Healing Yourself.* The former focuses on identifying and releasing burdens, while the latter centers on restoring balance and well-being in the body, mind, and spirit.

The 8 Ways of Giving It Back

The *8 Ways of Giving It Back* serve as guiding principles to help us **recognize and return false burdens, projections, and emotional weight** that we were never meant to carry. Each principle acts as a daily practice that fosters freedom and clarity. Here's a quick reminder of what the *8 Ways of Giving It Back* are:

1. **Boundary Acknowledgment – Clearly identifying what is yours and what is theirs.**

    o Many of us take on the weight of others' emotions, expectations, and struggles. Learning to **differentiate between our responsibilities and those belonging to others** helps us avoid emotional overload.

    o *Daily Application:* Start the day by asking, *"What is mine to carry today?"* If something belongs to someone else, visualize handing it back to them in your mind.

2. **Name It to Tame It – Recognizing the emotion or projection so you can give it back.**

    o Studies show that **naming emotions reduces their intensity** (Lieberman et al., 2007). Identifying when something is not yours to carry allows you to process and release it.

    o *Daily Application:* When feeling overwhelmed, take a deep breath and name the emotion aloud: *"This is not mine, and I give it back."*

3. **Reframing & Release Rituals – Simple practices like writing letters or performing symbolic acts.**

   o Expressing emotions through journaling or symbolic actions (like tearing up paper or burning old letters) allows for a **mental and emotional reset.**

   o *Daily Application:* Write down lingering stressors and say, *"I release this burden,"* as you discard or burn the note.

4. **Empathetic Detachment – Caring without carrying.**

   o Being compassionate does not mean absorbing others' pain. Practicing **detachment with love** helps us stay emotionally balanced.

   o *Daily Application:* Whenever you feel emotionally drained by someone's situation, remind yourself: *"I can support them without carrying their pain."*

5. **Prayer & Meditation – Spiritual tools to release and receive peace.**

   o Many spiritual traditions emphasize **surrendering anxieties to a higher power.** Studies show that **prayer and meditation reduce stress and improve well-being** (Kabat-Zinn, 1990).

   o *Daily Application:* Before bed, visualize placing all worries in God's hands and affirm, *"I trust in divine provision and protection."*

6. **Physical Realignment – Understanding how the body stores stress and tension.**

   o Trauma is stored in the body, especially in the **neck, shoulders, stomach, hips, and legs** (Van der Kolk, 2014).

   o *Daily Application:* Perform **body scans and movement exercises** to notice and release tension.

7. **Community Accountability – Surrounding yourself with people who recognize and support your boundaries.**

   o Healing is amplified through **support systems, faith-based groups, and mentorship.**

   o *Daily Application:* Check in with a trusted friend, therapist, or faith leader when you feel emotionally weighed down.

8. **Ongoing Maintenance – Daily check-ins and self-care strategies.**

   o Healing requires **consistent action**, including daily reflection and self-care.

   o *Daily Application:* End the day with **self-reflection**, asking, *"Did I carry something today that wasn't mine?"* and **release it before sleep.**

These 8 practices help us break free from false burdens and create emotional and spiritual space for healing. Now, let's explore how they integrate with *The 10 Methods of Healing Yourself.*

Pairing the 10 Methods of Healing with the 8 Ways of Giving It Back

The 10 Methods of Healing Yourself focus on the **body-centered approach to trauma release**, while the 8 Ways of Giving It Back provide the framework for **emotional and relational boundaries.** Below is a guide to integrating these methods into daily practice:

1. **Head & Neck (Releasing Mental Chatter) → Name It to Tame It**

    o **Morning Ritual:** Start your day with **spoken affirmations** and a **5-minute thought dump journal exercise** to clear mental clutter.

    o **Evening Practice:** Identify **negative self-talk or stress triggers** from the day and release them through prayer or meditation.

2. **Shoulders & Chest (Letting Go of Burdens) → Boundary Acknowledgment**

    o **Morning Ritual:** Stretch and breathe deeply, **setting your intention** for the day.

    o **Daily Practice:** If you notice tension in your shoulders, pause and **ask yourself, "Is this burden mine to carry?"** If not, give it back.

3. **Stomach & Diaphragm (Gut Feelings & Anxiety) → Reframing & Release Rituals**

   o **Daily Practice:** When you feel anxiety in your stomach, practice **diaphragmatic breathing** to calm the nervous system.

   o **Release Ritual:** Write down fears and burn or tear the paper as a **symbol of releasing them.**

4. **Pelvis & Hips (Emotional Stability & Movement) → Empathetic Detachment**

   o **Daily Practice:** Before engaging in emotional conversations, remind yourself: **"I can care without carrying."**

   o **Physical Exercise:** Move your hips through stretching or dance to **free stored emotions.**

5. **Legs & Feet (Grounding & Forward Movement) → Community Accountability**

   o **Morning Ritual:** Spend time **grounding outdoors** or walking barefoot for stability.

   o **Daily Practice:** Check in with **trusted friends, a mentor, or a faith-based community** for support.

By integrating these practices, we **reinforce the healing journey daily**, ensuring that trauma, stress, and false burdens do not become permanent residents in our body and mind.

You are not just healing; you are thriving. Continue to give back what is not yours, embrace what is, and walk boldly in your purpose.

FOOTNOTES

1. Lieberman, M. D. et al. (2007). *Putting feelings into words: Affect labeling disrupts amygdala activity in response to affective stimuli.* Psychological Science, 18(5), 421-428.

2. Kabat-Zinn, J. (1990). *Full catastrophe living: Using the wisdom of your body and mind to face stress, pain, and illness.* Delacorte.

3. Van der Kolk, B. (2014). *The body keeps the score: Brain, mind, and body in the healing of trauma.* Penguin Publishing Group.

CHAPTER 13

REAL-LIFE 'GIVE IT BACK' STORIES & TESTIMONIALS

O ne of the most powerful aspects of *The Give It Back Theory* is that it is **universal**. Whether you are a single parent, a business executive, a college student, or a retiree, we all carry burdens that were never meant for us. But once we learn to **identify them, release them, and reclaim our energy**, true transformation begins.

This chapter highlights real-life stories from friends, workshop attendees, and public figures who have embraced this concept and seen profound shifts in their lives. For privacy, each individual's name has been changed, but their experiences are real and their breakthroughs undeniable. These stories will inspire, encourage, and remind you that you are not alone—and that it is never too late to give back what was never yours.

From Burnout to Breakthrough: Beth's Story

Beth had spent years carrying the emotional weight of her family. As the fourth of eight siblings, she often found herself mediating family disputes, handling the emotional needs of her aging mother, and managing the expectations of her grown children and grandchildren. When her mother fell ill, Beth felt it was her responsibility to ensure everything was taken care of. The pressure mounted, and she began feeling exhausted, overwhelmed, and stuck in a cycle of never-ending caregiving.

But after attending a *Give It Back* workshop, Beth had a revelation:

"I realized I had confused love with responsibility. Loving my family didn't mean fixing everything for them."

She began setting clear boundaries, practicing empathetic detachment, and using journaling to release stress. Within six months, Beth reported feeling lighter, more energized, and more present in her own life.

Her biggest lesson?

"Giving it back doesn't mean giving up on people. It means trusting them to grow."

Breaking Generational Cycles: Donald's Journey

Donald carried the emotional weight of his father's untimely death, his youngest brother's tragic passing, and the high expectations of his older brother. After his father's passing, he felt it was his duty to step up, but his life spiraled into drug addiction and repeated jail sentences from his teens into adulthood.

During a one-on-one coaching session, Donald was asked a simple question: *"Whose emotional weight are you carrying?"*

His answer?

"I'm carrying my father's pain, my brother's pain, and my own shame. I never realized it wasn't mine to hold."

Donald began using *The 8 Ways of Giving It Back*, particularly naming and reframing. He practiced verbalizing emotions, attending therapy, and engaging in intentional healing work.

The result?

"I broke a generational cycle. I'm no longer carrying their pain as my own, and I'm free to build a future that isn't defined by my past."

The Politician Who Overcame Abandonment

A rising politician came to me during one of the most challenging times of his career. He was preparing for a higher office campaign, but the biggest hurdle wasn't his policies—it was the deep wounds left by friends and supporters who had abandoned him along the way.

His words were filled with frustration and pain:

"Every time I try to go to the next level, people leave. I feel like I can't trust anyone."

Through coaching, he realized that his success was never dependent on who stayed or who left. He started practicing prayer and release rituals, allowing himself to give back the fear of rejection and embrace his own worth.

"Now, I'm running my campaign with a new mindset. I'm not chasing approval—I'm walking in purpose."

Sometimes, *giving it back* means letting people go and knowing that your path is still valid, even when you walk it alone.

The Artist Who Found Her Voice Again

Rachel, an independent singer-songwriter, had spent years creating music that she felt would please others. She was afraid to create from her true emotions, worried about industry expectations and the fear of rejection.

After working through *The Give It Back Theory*, she started exploring who she was outside of external validation. She journaled through her creative blocks, released the burden of needing to be "perfect," and gave back the pressure placed on her by the industry.

Her transformation was evident. She shared:

"For the first time, I'm making music for me again. I don't feel chained by other people's opinions."

Not only did her creativity return, but she also saw success on her own terms, proving that authenticity leads to freedom.

The 'Overachiever's Anonymous' Academy

Many of us mistake busyness for purpose. We wear exhaustion like a badge of honor, believing that if we stop carrying everything for everyone, we will lose our worth.

But here's a revelation: You are already enough. Even when you do nothing.

Taking on too much is not an act of service—it's often an act of **self-neglect**. *Giving it back* isn't just about *what* you release, but also *who you become when you do*.

Ask yourself:

- Why am I so afraid to let go?
- Who am I when I'm not over-functioning?
- What would change if I gave myself permission to just *be*?

It's time to **graduate from The Overachiever's Academy and step into peace**.

Encouragement: It's Your Turn to Give It Back

If you take nothing else from this book, take this: **You are not responsible for carrying the world on your shoulders.** You were never meant to.

Healing is a daily practice, and giving it back is a spiritual discipline. **Your freedom is waiting on you.**

You don't have to be perfect. You don't have to have it all figured out. But you do have to start.

Closing Thoughts: The Deep Call to Action

Healing is not just an idea. It is not just something we read about and nod in agreement with. **It is a decision.**

It is the moment when you stand in front of everything you've ever carried and say, *"No more."* It is the moment when you choose to trust that you are worth more than the weight you've been dragging around.

Give it back.

To the childhood wounds, to the generational curses, to the toxic cycles, to the unrealistic expectations, to the lies you've believed about yourself—**give it back.**

Step into **freedom.** Step into **healing.** Step into the **life** you were created for.

Because on the other side of surrender is **wholeness.** And it's yours for the taking.

So, Beloved, **what will you give back today?**

CHAPTER 14

YOUR ONGOING JOURNEY—A CALL TO ACTION

You have walked through these pages, uncovering truths that have been buried under layers of obligation, guilt, and second-hand trauma. You have been challenged to give it back—to return the weight of burdens that were never yours to carry. And now, as you stand at the threshold of this journey, the question remains: **What will you do next?**

Healing is not a one-time decision; it is a daily practice, a lifelong commitment to freedom. You must choose daily to reclaim your peace, to stand in your power, and to live the life you were meant to live. This is your invitation to make *The Give It Back Theory* more than just words on a page—it is your invitation to live it, to embody it, and to share it with the world.

If You're Going to Win, You Have to Show Up With Only What's Yours

When young David arrived at the battlefield where the Israelites stood trembling before the Philistine giant, he was immediately met with expectations. His brothers questioned his presence, and King Saul, doubting his ability, tried to equip him with his own royal armor (1 Samuel 17:38-40). Saul assumed that if David was going to win against Goliath, he needed to wear something heavier, something more seasoned, something that belonged to another warrior. But David quickly realized something profound—he could not fight his battle in someone else's armor.

David took off the armor, gave it back, and chose to face Goliath only with what belonged to him—a sling, five smooth stones, and his faith.

If you're going to win your battle, you must show up to the field with only what belongs to you. You cannot fight in someone else's armor. You cannot carry someone else's expectations, burdens, or traumas and expect to move freely. Victory requires authenticity. It requires stepping into your own power, fully unburdened by what was never yours to carry.

Many of us have been walking around in armor that was never ours, weighed down by responsibilities, false identities, and other people's baggage. It's time to take it off. It's time to *give it back*.

Reflection: Are You Ready to Give It Back?

Pause for a moment and ask yourself:

- What burdens am I still holding onto that were never mine to carry?

- Have I internalized the pain, expectations, or disappointments of others?

- What relationships in my life need new boundaries?

- Am I ready to let go of the weight that has kept me stuck?

Your healing starts with awareness and continues with action. You have learned the *8 Ways of Giving It Back* and the *10 Methods of Healing Yourself*—now it is time to implement them daily.

The Spiritual Law of Giving and Receiving

Many of us are familiar with the verse:

"Give, and it will come back to you: good measure, pressed down, shaken together, and running over..." (Luke 6:38).

But what if this principle is not just about money and resources—what if it is also about emotional burdens?

When you give back to someone what was never yours to carry—their fears, their expectations, their emotional baggage—you are not abandoning them. You are actually giving them the opportunity to rise up and face their own giants. And in return, the same spiritual law applies to you: the moment you release what is not yours, you immediately create space to heal what is.

"The more you give, the more you shall receive" (Luke 6:38).

This is not just about generosity—it's about reciprocity and making space. You cannot receive healing if your hands are full of things that do not belong to you. When you give someone back their responsibility, their emotional weight, their trauma, you give them a gift—the opportunity to grow, to step up, and to take ownership of their own healing.

And in return, you receive the opportunity to finally face and heal what is yours.

This is the divine exchange that *The Give It Back Theory* offers—when you stop carrying what isn't yours, you make space for what is meant to make you whole.

Pass It Forward: Becoming an Advocate for Healing

What happens when you *give it back*? You don't just find relief for yourself—you create space for others to do the same. As you step into your healing, you naturally become an advocate for those still weighed down.

This message isn't just for you—it's for every person struggling under the emotional weight of false burdens.

You are now a carrier of this message. You have the power to change lives simply by sharing what you've learned.

Your Final Step: Take Action Today

If you've read this far, you are ready. **This is your moment to choose yourself.**

Here's how you can begin your ongoing journey:

1. **Commit to daily check-ins.** Every morning, ask yourself: *What am I carrying that isn't mine?* Every night, release what does not belong to you.

2. **Join the movement.** Follow my podcast, attend a workshop, or become part of a community that is dedicated to healing.

3. **Pass it forward.** Share your journey, teach these principles, and help others begin their own process of giving it back.

4. **Step into your calling.** Whatever dreams have been buried under the weight of false burdens—**it's time to reclaim them.**

A Closing Benediction: Your Freedom is Here

I leave you with this: **You were never created to carry the weight of the world.** You were meant to move freely, to walk lightly, to love deeply—without being crushed by the weight of what others have placed upon you.

There is a table set before you, a life of peace and purpose waiting for you. But you cannot sit at this table while carrying the weight of everything and everyone else.

It is time.

Time to give it back. Time to step into freedom. Time to reclaim what was always yours.

So, Beloved, I ask you one final time:

What will you give back today?

And when you answer, may you step forward into the lightness of a life fully, freely, and unapologetically your own.

THE END